WITNESS TO THE AGE OF REVOLUTION

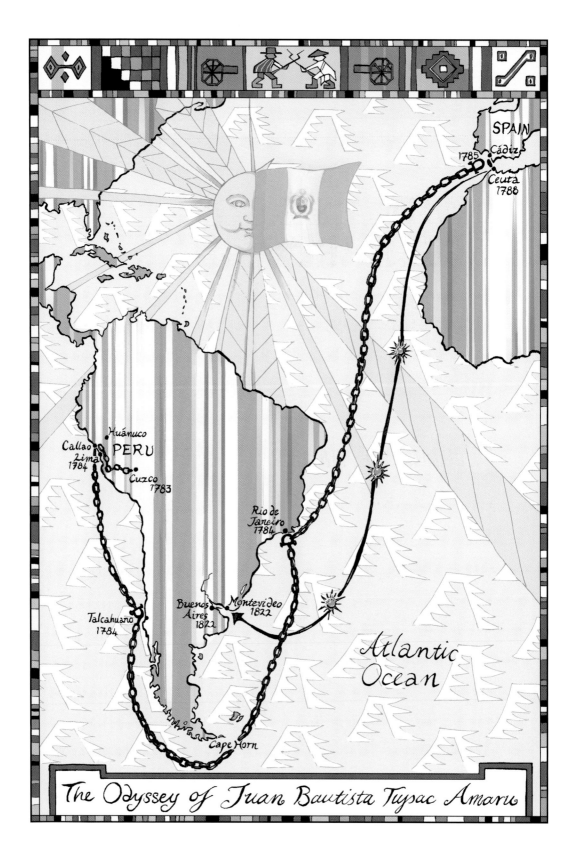

The Odyssey of Juan Bautista Tupac Amaru

WITNESS TO THE AGE OF REVOLUTION

THE ODYSSEY OF JUAN BAUTISTA TUPAC AMARU

CHARLES F. WALKER

LIZ CLARKE

OXFORD
UNIVERSITY PRESS

OXFORD
UNIVERSITY PRESS

Oxford University Press is a department of the University of Oxford. It furthers
the University's objective of excellence in research, scholarship, and education
by publishing worldwide. Oxford is a registered trade mark of Oxford University
Press in the UK and certain other countries.

Published in the United States of America by Oxford University Press
198 Madison Avenue, New York, NY 10016, United States of America.

Library of Congress Cataloging-in-Publication Data

Names: Túpac Amaru, Juan Bautista, 1742?–1827, author. |
    Walker, Charles F., 1959– author. | Clarke, Liz, 1982– illustrator.
Title: Witness to the age of revolution : the odyssey of Juan Bautista
    Tupac Amaru / Charles F. Walker and Liz Clarke.
Description: New York : Oxford University Press, [2020] |
    Includes bibliographical references. |
Identifiers: LCCN 2019050723 (print) | LCCN 2019050724 (ebook) |
    ISBN 9780190941154 (paperback) | ISBN 9780190941161 (pdf) |
    ISBN 9780190941178 (epub)
Subjects: LCSH: Túpac Amaru, Juan Bautista, 1742?–1827. |
    Political prisoners—Peru—Biography. | Peru—History—Insurrection of Tupac
    Amaru, 1780–1781. | Túpac Amaru, Juan Bautista, 1742?–1827—Comic books,
    strips, etc. | Political prisoners—Peru—Biography—Comic books, strips, etc. |
    Peru—History—Insurrection of Tupac Amaru, 1780–1781—Comic books, strips, etc.
Classification: LCC F3444 .T894 2020 (print) | LCC F3444 (ebook) |
    DDC 985/.033092 [B]—dc23
LC record available at https://lccn.loc.gov/2019050723
LC ebook record available at https://lccn.loc.gov/2019050724

9 8 7 6 5 4 3 2 1

Printed by LSC Communications, United States of America

To the memory of Juan Bautista Tupac Amaru and
Friar Marcos Durán Martel, for their inspiring resistance,
persistence, and loyalty to each other.

CONTENTS

PREFACE

Historians occasionally come across stories so fantastical that they surpass fiction. Such is the case with the tale of Juan Bautista Tupac Amaru, the subject of this graphic history. Influential readers deemed his memoirs, published in Buenos Aires at some point between 1824 and 1826, apocryphal—a fake. They could or would not believe that a half-brother of the famous Peruvian rebel martyr Tupac Amaru appeared in Argentina's capital forty years after the uprising with an incredible transatlantic tale of imprisonment, oppression, and salvation.

Erased by an incredulous audience of literary luminaries, Juan Bautista's story languished for over a century. Scholars only began to take him seriously with the 1941 publication of his memoirs in Peru. The editor, Francisco Loayza, showed that both Juan Bautista and *Forty Years of Captivity* were legitimate, including the claim that Juan Bautista was Tupac Amaru's half-brother and a descendent of the Incas. Loayza painstakingly proved that Juan Bautista was the author and underlined how the memoirs shed light on the era. Loayza's publication sparked interest in Juan Bautista. New editions of his memoirs were subsequently published in Peru, Chile, and Argentina. Nonetheless, many onlookers continued to dismiss his work. As a result, he is neither a national hero in Peru, nor has he claimed his rightful position as a universal symbol of resistance in the Age of Revolution.

In fairness to the skeptics, Juan Bautista was an unlikely icon. He did not lead men into battle or give inspiring speeches. His memoirs are his only publication. He himself expressed surprise at his turns of fate, including his decades of harsh imprisonment and his return to freedom in Argentina as an old man.

Born in 1747 in an indigenous area south of Cuzco, the heart of the Incan Empire, Juan Bautista was the half-brother of José Gabriel Condorcanqui Tupac Amaru, the leader, along with his wife Micaela Bastidas, of the massive rebellion that exploded across the Andes from 1780 to 1783. The rebels nearly defeated the Spanish and have become icons to groups ranging from independence fighters a couple decades later to twentieth-century guerrilla groups in Uruguay and Peru. The rapper Tupac Shakur was named after José Gabriel. The Tupac Amaru brothers descended from the Inca monarchs defeated by the Spanish in the sixteenth century.

Juan Bautista participated in the uprising but did not occupy a leadership role. Among other allegations, prosecutors charged him with carrying his brother's bed. He was arrested and, to his surprise, released. He and his wife Susana Aguirre were then arrested again in 1782, during the brutal repression against anyone related to Tupac Amaru. Executioners had tortured and quartered his brother in a grisly public ritual on May 18, 1781. They used the garrote on Bastidas and hanged other family members and members of their inner circle.

After a horrendous year in a Cuzco jail, Juan Bautista's "odyssey," as he called it, began in 1783. He was transported in shackles across the Andes to Lima. His tribulations included watching his mother die of dehydration while guards stood by and refused to help. He spent time in a claustrophobic and unhealthy cell in the San Felipe Fort in Callao, where he and many of his comrades contracted malaria, and was sentenced to exile in Spain. Juan Bautista and the other prisoners suffered during the journey around Cape Horn and across the Atlantic. More than half of the prisoners perished, including Susana Aguirre.

In 1788, after three years in the San Sebastián Castle in Cádiz, authorities sent Juan Bautista to the Ceuta presidio (a garrisoned fort and penal colony) in northern Africa, across from Gibraltar. He would spend more than thirty years in this Spanish outpost in Morocco. News of insurgencies exploding across the globe periodically raised his hopes for freedom, but they were repeatedly dashed. He befriended veterans and prisoners from Spain's conflicts with Napoleon's France, England, and independence forces in the Americas. He heard stories and debated about the French and Haitian Revolutions, Trafalgar, Napoleon's invasion of Iberia, and the wars of independence in Spanish America. The emergence of Liberalism in Spain, whose leaders—in contrast to the Absolutist Conservatives they replaced—considered Tupac Amaru and thousands of others to be political prisoners, ultimately led to his freedom in 1820. Since 1813, he had enjoyed the company and support of another Peruvian political prisoner, Augustinian friar Marcos Durán Martel. Their love and dedication to each another is heartwarming. After many crushing disappointments, from bureaucratic (he had been in jail so long that amnesties handed down by officials did not cover him) to physical (he fell and broke his arm leaving Ceuta), he and Durán Martel reached Argentina in 1822. Juan Bautista was seventy-five years old.

To his amazement, he was a hero in Argentina, which had defeated the Spanish but had not yet consolidated as a nation. Many independence leaders had cast the Incas as part of Argentina's "usable past," as historic figures who provided inspiration in the present, and even considered Juan Bautista a potential king. Furthermore, he had befriended many Spanish American independence heroes in Ceuta. The governor of Buenos Aires, Bernardino Rivadavia, granted Juan Bautista and Durán Martel pensions and room and board on the condition that Juan Bautista write his memoirs. They were published in Buenos Aires but to no great fanfare. He died in Buenos Aires in 1827, having never returned to Peru.

Juan Bautista had a ringside seat to the events of the Age of Revolution and rubbed shoulders with many of the era's important figures. After fighting in the Tupac Amaru Rebellion, he met an amazing cast of prisoners in Cádiz and Ceuta: Spanish Americans, Spaniards, Europeans, and a variety of political dissidents, who would later play important roles in securing his freedom. He also befriended veterans of the French Revolution, the Napoleonic Wars, and other popular uprisings. Moreover, Ceuta not only received prisoners but also sent sailors to fight against the British in battles such as Trafalgar in 1805. From Ceuta, prisoners such as Juan Bautista could follow naval movements and other news on the Mediterranean and the Atlantic; sailors, soldiers, and others passed along and debated news, stories, and rumors, keeping them apprised of events in France, Spain, Morocco, and beyond. He witnessed the rise, fall, and return of Liberalism in Spain and the consolidation of Argentina as an independent republic.

Why did some writers doubt the veracity of his story? On one hand, even the most creative author would struggle to invent these transatlantic travails of a descendent of the Incas, with all the twists and turns and bitter disappointments Juan Bautista described. As several authors have noted, the memoirs read like an Andean *Count of Monte Cristo*, Alexandre Dumas *père*'s 1844 novel of wrongful imprisonment, harrowing escapes from jail, and revenge. Meanwhile, many readers doubted that an indigenous man with little formal education could have written such stirring memoirs. The doubts reflected racist assumptions about authorship and education. Ever since the 1820s, conservative authors seeking to downplay the importance of the Tupac Amaru Rebellion or to torpedo the work of an indigenous political prisoner have dismissed Juan Bautista. This graphic history underscores the ways in which he educated himself with the help of Father Durán Martel and others and received their assistance in writing his memoirs, a common practice of shared authorship in the nineteenth century.

Juan Bautista's fascinating and painful story moves from one beautiful and majestic city and port to another: Cuzco, Lima, Rio de Janeiro, Cádiz, Ceuta, and Buenos Aires. A graphic treatment allows readers to see these places where he was forcibly transported and to understand their roles in the Age of Revolution. Instead of fictionalizing his life, I have allowed images, drawn from archival materials, to tell the story. I want to chronicle his story but not speak for Juan Bautista Tupac Amaru, whose first language was

Quechua. Juan Bautista's harrowing, marvelous tale is a remarkable one of survival and personal transformation, as he evolved from a secondary figure in his brother's revolution to a symbol of colonial oppression and, after many decades, freedom. It also sheds light on events in the Americas and Europe in an era of rapid change.

GRAPHIC HISTORY SERIES

Widely acclaimed by educators, the award-winning Graphic History Series introduces students to the ways that historians construct the past. Going beyond simply depicting events in the past, each title in the Graphic History Series combines the power of imagery with primary sources, historical essays, and cutting-edge historiography to offer a powerful tool for teaching history and teaching *about* history.

PUBLISHED

Trevor R. Getz and Liz Clarke, *Abina and the Important Men*

Ronald Schechter and Liz Clarke, *Mendoza the Jew: Boxing, Manliness, and Nationalism*

Rafe Blaufarb and Liz Clarke, *Inhuman Traffick: The International Struggle Against the Transatlantic Slave Trade*

Nina Caputo and Liz Clarke, *Debating Truth: The Barcelona Disputation of 1263*

Andrew Kirk and Kristian Purcell, *Doom Towns: The People and Landscapes of Atomic Testing*

Jennifer A. Rea and Liz Clarke, *Perpetua's Journey: Faith, Gender, & Power in the Roman Empire*

Michael G. Vann and Liz Clarke, *The Great Hanoi Rat Hunt: Empire, Disease, and Modernity in French Colonial Vietnam*

Karlos K. Hill and Dave Dodson, *The Murder of Emmett Till*

Charles F. Walker and Liz Clarke, *Witness to the Age of Revolution: The Odyssey of Juan Bautista Tupac Amaru*

FORTHCOMING

Bryan McCann and Gilmar Fraga, *The Black Lancers and the Ragamuffin Revolt*

Maura Elizabeth Cunningham and Liz Clarke, *Wandering Lives: Art and Politics in Twentieth-Century China*

PART I
THE GRAPHIC HISTORY

CHAPTER 1

THE TUPAC AMARU REBELLION

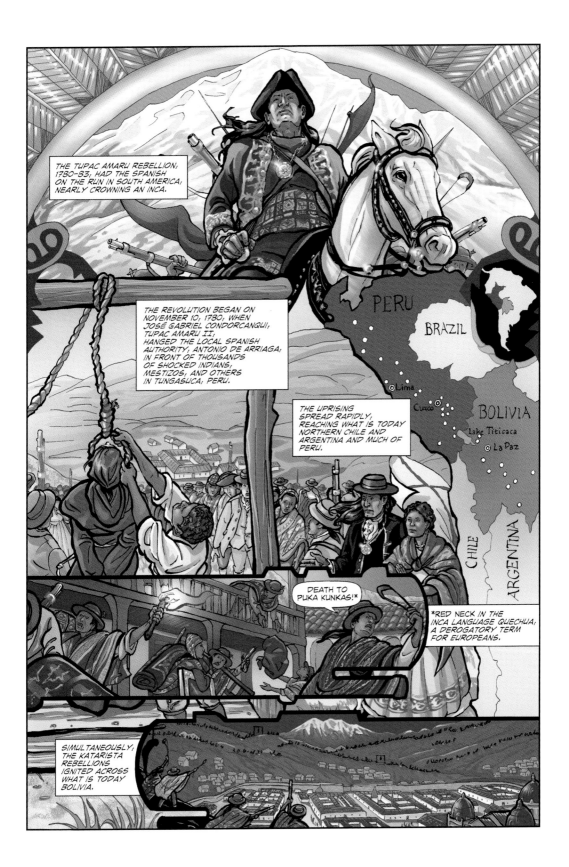

THE TUPAC AMARU REBELLION, 1780-83, HAD THE SPANISH ON THE RUN IN SOUTH AMERICA, NEARLY CROWNING AN INCA.

THE REVOLUTION BEGAN ON NOVEMBER 10, 1780, WHEN JOSÉ GABRIEL CONDORCANQUI, TUPAC AMARU II, HANGED THE LOCAL SPANISH AUTHORITY, ANTONIO DE ARRIAGA, IN FRONT OF THOUSANDS OF SHOCKED INDIANS, MESTIZOS, AND OTHERS IN TUNGASUCA, PERU.

THE UPRISING SPREAD RAPIDLY, REACHING WHAT IS TODAY NORTHERN CHILE AND ARGENTINA AND MUCH OF PERU.

PERU

BRAZIL

Lima

Cuzco

BOLIVIA

Lake Titicaca

La Paz

CHILE

ARGENTINA

DEATH TO PUKA KUNKAS!*

*RED NECK IN THE INCA LANGUAGE QUECHUA, A DEROGATORY TERM FOR EUROPEANS.

SIMULTANEOUSLY, THE KATARISTA REBELLIONS IGNITED ACROSS WHAT IS TODAY BOLIVIA.

5

JOSÉ GABRIEL CONDORCANQUI, WHO USED HIS INCA PATRONYM TUPAC AMARU, AND HIS WIFE MICAELA BASTIDAS LED THE REBELLION.

TUPAC WAS DESCENDED FROM ONE OF THE LAST INCAS, EXECUTED BY THE SPANISH IN 1572.

TUPAC AMARU REPRESENTED HIS TOWNS AS A KURAKA (ETHNIC AUTHORITY) AND WORKED AS A MERCHANT-MULETEER.

MICAELA RAN THEIR BUSINESS WHEN HE WAS RUNNING MULES TO THE POTOSÍ MINES AND JUJUY (ARGENTINA), GIVING HER IMPORTANT LOGISTIC SKILLS FOR THE REBELLION.

HAKU RUNAKUNA, HAKUYÁ.*

*LET'S GET GOING PEOPLE; GO, GO, GO.

THEY SPOKE QUECHUA, THE INCA LANGUAGE, TODAY SPOKEN BY MORE THAN 10 MILLION PEOPLE.

*INCA REVIVALISM

*COLONIAL NOTIONS OF "GOOD GOVERNMENT"

*SOME ELEMENTS OF THE ENLIGHTENMENT

MOST ANALYSTS UNDERLINE MASS OPPOSITION TO THE "BOURBON REFORMS" AS THE UNDERLYING CAUSE. THESE WERE MEASURES BY THE SPANISH TO INCREASE REVENUE AND CONTROL IN THEIR AMERICAN COLONIES.

TUPAC AMARU'S HALF-BROTHER, JUAN BAUTISTA, WROTE THIS EXPLANATION IN THE 1820S, IN HIS MEMOIRS:

King Charles III sent a commissioner named José Antonio de Areche, with the title of Visitador, to establish state monopolies, custom houses, sales taxes etc. throughout Peru. These rapacious measures by the Spanish, opening the doors to their greed, set off the desperation of the indigenous people.

On October 4, 1780 my brother put himself at the head of 25,000 Indians.

TUPAC AMARU AND MICAELA BASTIDAS SOUGHT A MULTI-ETHNIC ALLIANCE BUT OVER TIME IT BECAME A VIRTUAL CASTE WAR, INDIANS AGAINST EUROPEANS.

MICAELA BASTIDAS WAS NOT THE ONLY FEMALE LEADER. TOMASA TITO CONDEMAYTA, THE KURAKA OF ACOS, LED TROOPS IN NUMEROUS BATTLES.

THE ROYALISTS, AFTER NEAR DEFEAT IN THE SNOW-COVERED PEAKS, PUSHED AHEAD. IN APRIL 1781, THEY CAPTURED TUPAC AMARU WHEN TWO OF HIS MEN BETRAYED HIM.

DAYS LATER THEY CAPTURED MICAELA AND MUCH BUT NOT ALL OF THEIR FAMILY.

THE SPANISH EXECUTED TUPAC AMARU, MICAELA BASTIDAS, AND THEIR INNER CIRCLE ON MAY 18, 1781.

THE PEOPLE OF CUZCO WATCHED STUNNED AS EXECUTIONERS USED ROPES, HORSES, THE GARROTE, AND EVEN KNIVES TO MAXIMIZE THE PAIN AND SPECTACLE.

THEIR SON FERNANDO, AGE 10, WAS FORCED TO WITNESS THE SLOW DEATHS OF HIS PARENTS AND BROTHER.

Nooooooooo

THE UPRISING IS NOW OVER.

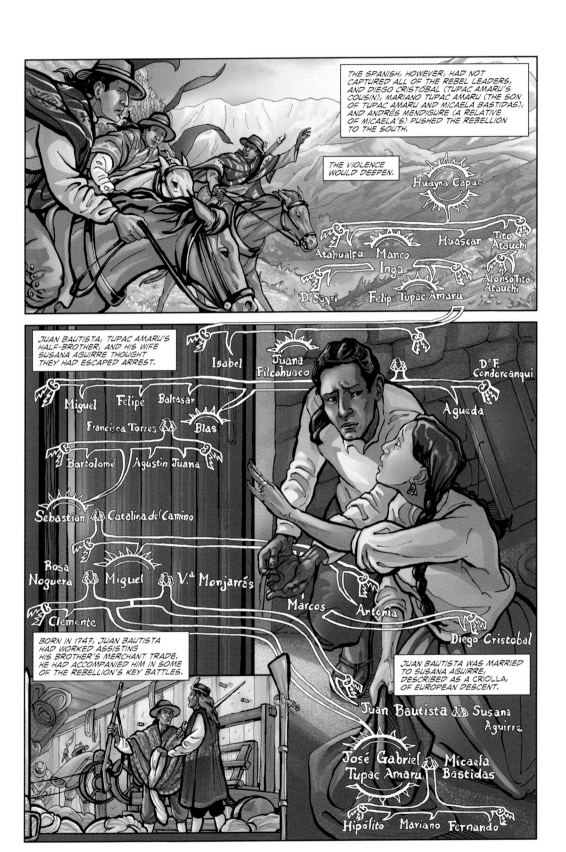

THE SPANISH, HOWEVER, HAD NOT CAPTURED ALL OF THE REBEL LEADERS, AND DIEGO CRISTÓBAL (TUPAC AMARU'S COUSIN), MARIANO TUPAC AMARU (THE SON OF TUPAC AMARU AND MICAELA BASTIDAS), AND ANDRÉS MENDIGURE (A RELATIVE OF MICAELA'S) PUSHED THE REBELLION TO THE SOUTH.

THE VIOLENCE WOULD DEEPEN.

Huayna Capac

Atahualpa   Manco Inga   Huascar   Tito Atauchi

D. Sayri   Felipe Tupac Amaru   Alonso Tito Atauchi

JUAN BAUTISTA, TUPAC AMARU'S HALF-BROTHER, AND HIS WIFE SUSANA AGUIRRE THOUGHT THEY HAD ESCAPED ARREST.

Isabel   Juana Pilcohuaco   D. F. Condorcanqui

Miguel   Felipe   Baltasar   Agueda

Francisca Torres   Blas

Bartolomé   Agustín Juana

Sebastian   Catalina del Camino

Rosa Noguera   Miguel   V.ª Monjarrás

Marcos   Antonia

Clemente

Diego Cristobal

BORN IN 1747, JUAN BAUTISTA HAD WORKED ASSISTING HIS BROTHER'S MERCHANT TRADE. HE HAD ACCOMPANIED HIM IN SOME OF THE REBELLION'S KEY BATTLES.

JUAN BAUTISTA WAS MARRIED TO SUSANA AGUIRRE, DESCRIBED AS A CRIOLLA, OF EUROPEAN DESCENT.

Juan Bautista   Susana Aguirre

José Gabriel Tupac Amaru   Micaela Bastidas

Hipólito   Mariano   Fernando

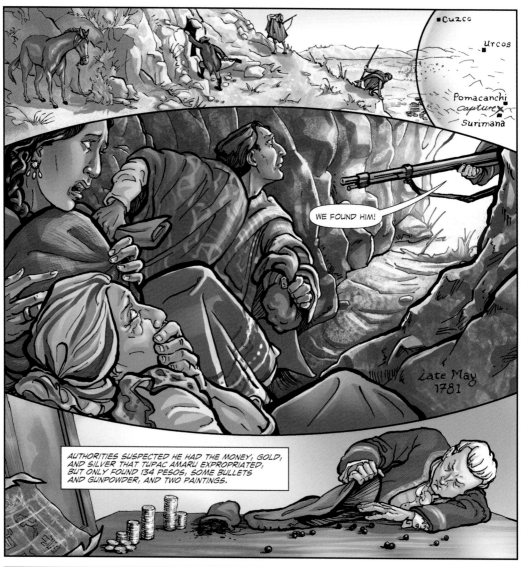

WE FOUND HIM!

AUTHORITIES SUSPECTED HE HAD THE MONEY, GOLD, AND SILVER THAT TUPAC AMARU EXPROPRIATED, BUT ONLY FOUND 134 PESOS, SOME BULLETS AND GUNPOWDER, AND TWO PAINTINGS.

FOR AIDING YOUR BROTHER, YOU ARE SENTENCED TO 200 LASHES AND 10 YEARS OF JAIL IN THE SAN JUAN DE ULÚA CASTLE IN MEXICO.

GUARDS AND OTHERS MISTREATED JUAN BAUTISTA IN JAIL. HE WAS NOT SENT TO MEXICO.

REBEL HERETIC!

IN HIS MEMOIRS, JUAN BAUTISTA LAMENTED THAT WHILE SOME INDIANS LOOKED AT HIM WITH COMPASSION, OTHERS MIMICKED THE SPANIARDS' CRUELTY.

Spanish ferocity had been spread almost by contagion to the Indians themselves, naturally humane and sweet... some who saw me on the street at times risked giving me a compassionate look; those who had become soldiers, if they didn't insult me with haughtiness, took on an unbearable air of disdain.

ALTHOUGH THE REBELLION CONTINUED, JUAN BAUTISTA AND SUSANA AGUIRRE RECEIVED PARDONS IN EARLY 1782.

11

CHAPTER 2
VIA CRUCIS

THE REBELLION MOVED TO THE SOUTH AND BECAME EVEN MORE VIOLENT.

OUR HOLD ON THE ANDES IS SHAKY— WE COULD LOSE.

16

IN SEPTEMBER, AUTHORITIES ORDERED THAT
78 PRISONERS, INCLUDING 61 FAMILY MEMBERS,
BE SENT FOR FURTHER TRIALS IN LIMA:
17 CHILDREN, 35 WOMEN, 26 MEN.

6,000 PEOPLE
WATCHED THE
PROCESSION.

RASCALS,
TRAITORS,
YOU SHOULD
PAY FOR IT!

TAKE MY HORSE,
YOU'LL NEED IT.

JUAN BAUTISTA DID NOT HAVE TIME
TO THANK THIS STRANGER, WHOSE
GIFT WOULD PROVE SO VALUABLE
IN THE LONG JOURNEY TO LIMA.

ALREADY WEAK FROM JAIL, THE PRISONERS SUFFERED GREATLY ON THE JOURNEY; A VIRTUAL DEATH MARCH.

WATER, WATER...

JUAN BAUTISTA WATCHED HIS MOTHER, VENTURA MONJARRÁS, DIE OF DEHYDRATION.

SOME PRISONERS COULDN'T BEAR THE JOURNEY.

THEY REACHED LIMA ON NOVEMBER 22, 1783.

San Lorenzo Island

Callao

Lima

LIMA WAS THE POLITICAL, ECONOMIC, AND RELIGIOUS CENTER OF PERU. ITS BAROQUE ARCHITECTURE, ACTIVE SOCIAL LIFE, AND MULTIRACIAL POPULATION CAPTIVATED VISITORS.

JUAN BAUTISTA AND OTHER MALE PRISONERS, HOWEVER, WERE HOUSED IN A DUNGEON IN THE RECENTLY BUILT REAL FELIPE FORT, IN THE NEARBY PORT OF CALLAO.

CHAPTER 3
ACROSS THE ATLANTIC

WORKERS LOADED THE EL PERUANO AND THE SAN PEDRO DE ALCÁNTARA WARSHIPS FOR THE LONG JOURNEY TO CÁDIZ, SPAIN NOT ONLY WITH PRISONERS AND OTHER PASSENGERS BUT ALSO A DANGEROUS AMOUNT OF PRECIOUS METALS: HUNDREDS OF TONS OF SILVER, COPPER, AND GOLD.

ALTHOUGH THE PEACE OF PARIS (1783) HAD ENDED THE AMERICAN REVOLUTIONARY WAR (SPAIN HAD SIDED WITH FRANCE AND THE EMERGING UNITED STATES AGAINST GREAT BRITAIN), SPAIN STILL FEARED THAT GREAT BRITAIN WOULD SEIZE SHIPS ON THE ATLANTIC.

THE SPANISH CAPTAIN JOSÉ DE CÓRDOVA WAS IN CHARGE OF EL PERUANO, A 60-CANNON MAN-OF-WAR.

ON APRIL 1, 1784, 21 PASSENGERS, THE CREW, AND 29 PRISONERS, INCLUDING JUAN BAUTISTA, SUSANA AGUIRRE, AND MARIANO CONDORCANQUI (SON OF JOSÉ GABRIEL AND MICAELA BASTIDAS), BOARDED EL PERUANO.

TAKE THAT, REBEL SCUM.

GUARDS ESCORTED FERNANDO TUPAC AMARU, ANDRÉS MENDIGURE, AND OTHER REBELS AND FAMILY MEMBERS ONTO THE SAN PEDRO DE ALCANTARÁ.

THE TWO SHIPS DEPARTED ON APRIL 13.

AMONG THE PASSENGERS ON EL PERUANO WAS THE DISTINGUISHED FRENCH BOTANIST JOSEPH DOMBEY.

BONJOUR, DR. DOMBEY.

IF YOU KEEP COMPLAINING, WE'LL TIE YOU ALL TO THE CANNONS.

BAD WEATHER BATTERED THE OVERLOADED SHIPS. THE ALCÁNTARA HAD TO PORT IN TALCAHUANO, CHILE FOR REPAIRS, SEPARATING THE TWO SHIPS, WHILE EL PERUANO SUFFERED FROM LEAKS.

YOU'LL GET YOUR MONEY.

PROFESSOR DOMBEY PAID RELUCTANT CREWMEMBERS TO DIVE INTO THE ICY WATER TO PATCH THE HULL.

28

30

THE PRISONERS SPENT FOUR MISERABLE MONTHS IN RIO.

During the day we were tied to the main mast and at night, the walkway; the rain, the relentless sun, our ragged clothes....

LET THEM WASH THESE RAGS FOR THE LOVE OF GOD.

AFTER 4 MONTHS EL PERUANO DEPARTED RIO FOR MONTEVIDEO AND THEN CÁDIZ.

THE CREW WORRIED THAT AN ENGLISH SHIP MIGHT SEIZE THE PRECIOUS METAL AND LIBERATE THE PRISONERS. THEY TIED THEM TO THE MAIN MAST.

They were all furious at us, the guards always menaced us with their bayonets, ready to run them through us; that was their language; they enjoyed watching us suffer with the water, the heat, the cold, our bodies almost naked, always thirsty and hungry.

EAT THIS.

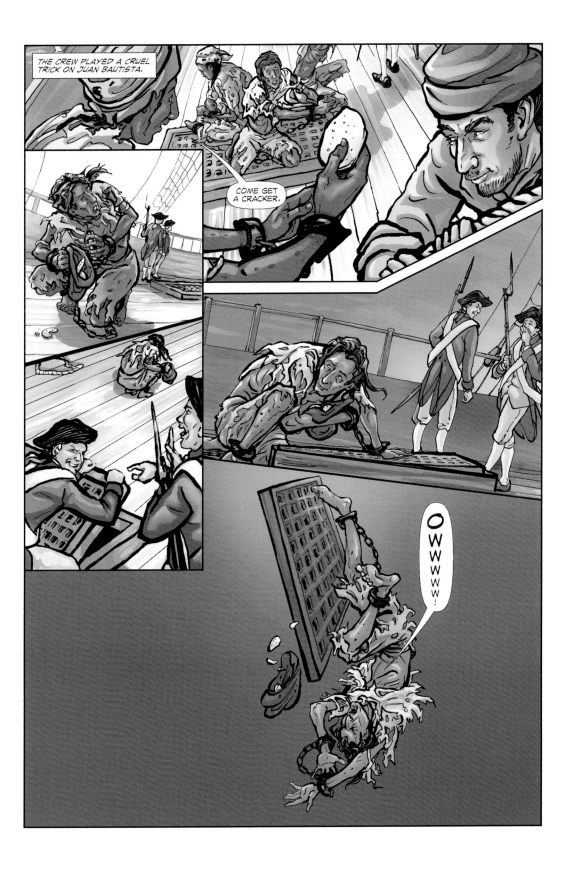

34

March 1 1785

Peniche

Lisbon

PORTUGAL

SPAIN

Cádiz

Atlantic
Ocean

Gibraltar

Ceuta

CÁDIZ!

Cádiz

Castillo
de
San Sebastián

AUTHORITIES WOULDN'T
PROCESS THE PRISONERS
UNTIL THEIR OFFICIAL
PAPERS ARRIVED, WHICH
WERE ON THE ALCÁNTARA.
IT HAD SUFFERED NUMEROUS
BREAKDOWNS AND WAS
ALMOST A YEAR BEHIND.

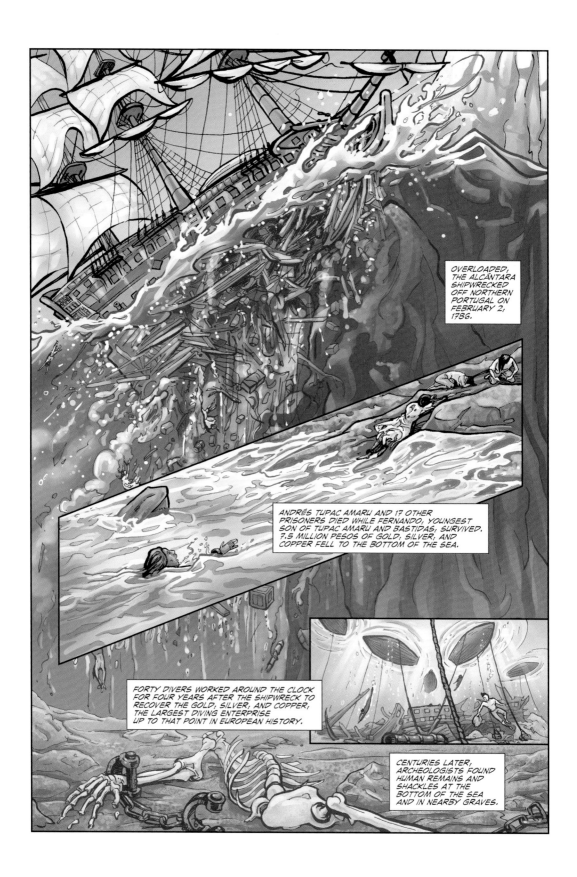

OVERLOADED, THE ALCÁNTARA SHIPWRECKED OFF NORTHERN PORTUGAL ON FEBRUARY 2, 1786.

ANDRÉS TUPAC AMARU AND 17 OTHER PRISONERS DIED WHILE FERNANDO, YOUNGEST SON OF TUPAC AMARU AND BASTIDAS, SURVIVED. 7.5 MILLION PESOS OF GOLD, SILVER, AND COPPER FELL TO THE BOTTOM OF THE SEA.

FORTY DIVERS WORKED AROUND THE CLOCK FOR FOUR YEARS AFTER THE SHIPWRECK TO RECOVER THE GOLD, SILVER, AND COPPER, THE LARGEST DIVING ENTERPRISE UP TO THAT POINT IN EUROPEAN HISTORY.

CENTURIES LATER, ARCHEOLOGISTS FOUND HUMAN REMAINS AND SHACKLES AT THE BOTTOM OF THE SEA AND IN NEARBY GRAVES.

Mariano Condorcanqui
(Phelipe Gonzales Tirnaycocayne)
(Mariano Barrera)
Bartolomé Guamán
Miguel Gutiérrez
Isidro Pérez
Pedro Nolasco Zimbrón
Joseph Mamani
(Antonio Grumusset)
Pascual Guamán
Nicolás Vitorino
Francisco Ruano
Mateo Condori
Josef Sánchez
(Don Blas Laso)
(Manuel Tito)
Cayetano Castro

Juan Tupac Amaru

Antonia de Castro
Andrea Juscamayta
Gregoria Mallqui
Nicolasa Torres
Susana Aguirre

(Mariano Tito)
Gregorio Tito
Juliana Tito
Maria Tito
(Miguel Tito)
Feliciana Tito

OF THE TWENTY-NINE PRISONERS
THAT LEFT LIMA IN 1784
ON EL PERUANO, EIGHTEEN DIED
EN ROUTE AND SEVEN MORE
IN PRISON IN CÁDIZ.
ONLY FOUR WERE ALIVE IN 1788.

GUARDS DRAPED A 25-POUND
CHAIN AROUND JUAN BAUTISTA.
TWO GUARDS HAD TO HELP
CARRY HIM OFF THE BOAT.

ONCE AGAIN, THE END
OF A BRUTAL JOURNEY
DID NOT MEAN THAT
HIS TROUBLES AND
AFFLICTIONS WERE OVER.

CHAPTER 4

ACROSS THE MEDITERRANEAN: CÁDIZ AND CEUTA

CÁDIZ WAS SPAIN'S MAJOR SOUTHERN PORT, A HUB FOR SHIPS TO THE AMERICAS. IT IS ARGUABLY THE OLDEST CONTINUOUSLY POPULATED CITY IN WESTERN EUROPE, FOUNDED BY THE PHOENICIANS.

San Sebastián Castle

JUAN BAUTISTA WAS TAKEN TO THE SAN SEBASTIÁN CASTLE.

HIS CELL WAS

destructive...all stone, with a small opening with a steel rod running across it; the floor was cobblestone and humid; double doors... with sheepskin and a bag of rags as my bed.

GUARDS STOOD AT THE DOOR, BY THE OPENING, AND ABOVE THE ROOM.

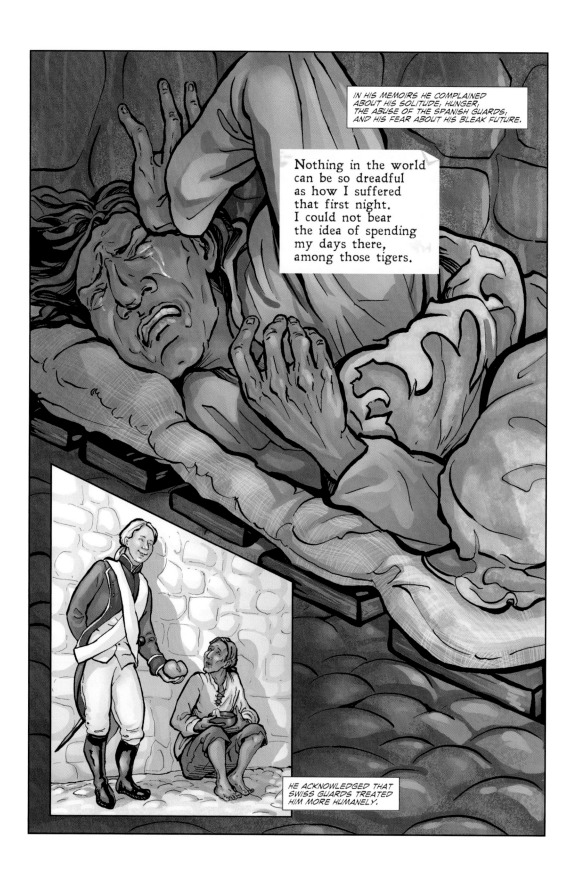

IN HIS MEMOIRS HE COMPLAINED ABOUT HIS SOLITUDE, HUNGER, THE ABUSE OF THE SPANISH GUARDS, AND HIS FEAR ABOUT HIS BLEAK FUTURE.

Nothing in the world can be so dreadful as how I suffered that first night. I could not bear the idea of spending my days there, among those tigers.

HE ACKNOWLEDGED THAT SWISS GUARDS TREATED HIM MORE HUMANELY.

43

CÁDIZ TO ISLA DE LEÓN, CHANGED SHIPS, THEN TO SANCTI PETRI, TO CEUTA, WHERE HE ARRIVED ON JUNE 1, 1788.

Cádiz
Isla de León
Sancti Petri
Algeciras
Gibraltar
Ceuta
Atlantic Ocean

Mediterranean Sea

JUAN BAUTISTA WOULD SPEND NEARLY 23 YEARS IN CEUTA...

...8.5 MILES FROM SOUTHERN SPAIN, ACROSS THE STRAIT OF GIBRALTAR. CEUTA'S MONTE HACHO AND GIBRALTAR MAKE UP "THE PILLARS OF HERCULES."

CEUTA

GIBRALTAR

ATLANTIC OCEAN
STRAIT OF GIBRALTAR
MEDITERRANEAN SEA

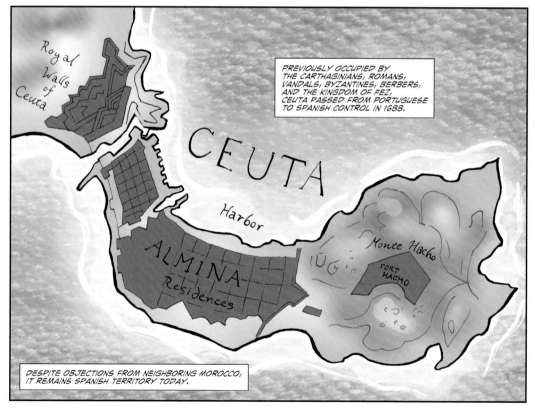

Royal Walls of Ceuta

PREVIOUSLY OCCUPIED BY THE CARTHAGINIANS, ROMANS, VANDALS, BYZANTINES, BERBERS, AND THE KINGDOM OF FEZ, CEUTA PASSED FROM PORTUGUESE TO SPANISH CONTROL IN 1688.

CEUTA

Harbor

Monte Hacho

FORT HACHO

ALMINA
Residences

DESPITE OBJECTIONS FROM NEIGHBORING MOROCCO, IT REMAINS SPANISH TERRITORY TODAY.

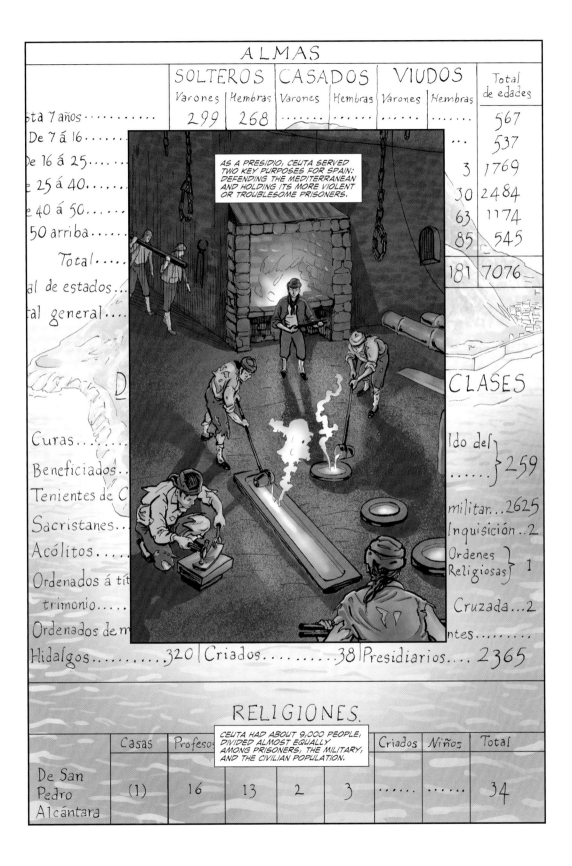

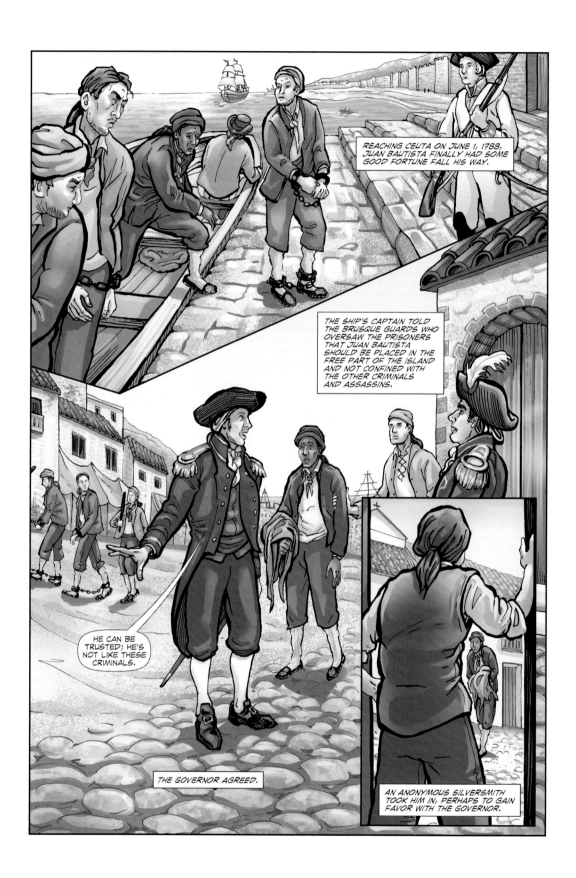

REACHING CEUTA ON JUNE 1, 1788, JUAN BAUTISTA FINALLY HAD SOME GOOD FORTUNE FALL HIS WAY.

THE SHIP'S CAPTAIN TOLD THE BRUSQUE GUARDS WHO OVERSAW THE PRISONERS THAT JUAN BAUTISTA SHOULD BE PLACED IN THE FREE PART OF THE ISLAND AND NOT CONFINED WITH THE OTHER CRIMINALS AND ASSASSINS.

HE CAN BE TRUSTED; HE'S NOT LIKE THESE CRIMINALS.

THE GOVERNOR AGREED.

AN ANONYMOUS SILVERSMITH TOOK HIM IN, PERHAPS TO GAIN FAVOR WITH THE GOVERNOR.

THE SILVERSMITH AND HIS WIFE
TREATED HIM POORLY.
JUAN BAUTISTA COMPLAINED
THAT HE SLEPT WHEREVER
HE COULD FIND A TINY SPACE.

PUT YOUR
RAGS DOWN THERE,
IN THE CORNER.

GET UP,
YOU LAZY
CRIMINAL.

JUAN BAUTISTA WORKED FOR
THE SILVERSMITH AND OTHERS
TO PAY HIS ROOM AND BOARD.

HE FINALLY ASKED TO LEAVE.

I WANT TO LIVE ALONE.

AUTHORITIES ALLOWED HIM TO MOVE TO A ROOM WITH A SMALL PLOT OF LAND. HE LIVED OFF THE SMALL STIPEND GRANTED TO ALL PRISONERS AND BY GROWING PRODUCE AND WORKING AT ODD JOBS.

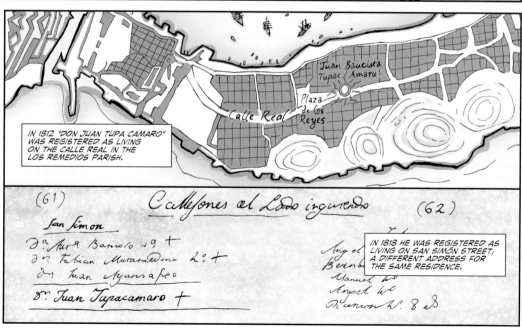

IN 1812 "DON JUAN TUPA CAMARO" WAS REGISTERED AS LIVING ON THE CALLE REAL IN THE LOS REMEDIOS PARISH.

IN 1818 HE WAS REGISTERED AS LIVING ON SAN SIMÓN STREET, A DIFFERENT ADDRESS FOR THE SAME RESIDENCE.

HE APPEARED IN ONE COURT DOCUMENT IN THE LATE 1780S WHEN HE TESTIFIED IN A CASE ABOUT DOMESTIC VIOLENCE.

HE EXPLAINED THAT HE WAS HAVING DINNER WITH A FRIEND, JOSEF ESCUDERO, WHEN THEY HEARD SHOUTS.

HE'S KILLING HER!

THEY RUSHED TO HELP AND SAW A MAN NAMED TORNERO RUN OUT HALF NAKED.

THEY AIDED HIS WIFE, WHO HAD INJURIES.

JUAN BAUTISTA'S NEAT SIGNATURE IN THE COURT DOCUMENTS INDICATES THAT HE WAS LITERATE.

49

50

AND CEUTA WAS DIFFICULT FOR EVERYONE. IT WAS OVERCROWDED, UNHEALTHY, AND VIOLENT.

OFFICIALS MADE MONEY IN MANY CORRUPT WAYS.

GUARDS WORRIED THAT PRISONERS WOULD ESCAPE TO MOROCCO AND EVEN CONVERT TO ISLAM.

WHAT BROKE THE TEDIUM OF DAILY LIFE WAS CEUTA'S IMPORTANT PLACE IN THE CHANGES TAKING PLACE IN SPAIN AND THE MEDITERRANEAN IN THE AGE OF REVOLUTIONS.

THESE DRASTICALLY ALTERED JUAN BAUTISTA'S LIFE.

ALTHOUGH LIFE IN THE WALLED-OFF PRESIDIO COULD BE TEDIOUS AND DAILY LIFE WAS TOUGH, JUAN BAUTISTA RUBBED ELBOWS WITH PARTICIPANTS IN WORLD-CHANGING EVENTS.

Cortes of Cádiz (Spanish National Assembly) 1810-1814

Latin American Wars of Independence 1808-1825

Moroccan Siege of Ceuta 1790-1791

French Invasion of Iberia (Peninsula Wars) 1808-1814

French Revolution 1789-1799

Spanish Constitution (Liberal) 1812

Argentina Independent 1816

Haitian Revolution 1791-1804

Absolutist Restoration (Ferdinand VII) 1814

Peru Independent 1821

Tupac Amaru Rebellion 1780-1783

Napoleonic Wars 1792-1815

Spain's Liberal Revolution 1810

American Revolution 1775-1783

THE SPANISH WORRIED ABOUT THE DIVERSE PEOPLE WHO SURROUNDED CEUTA IN NORTHERN AFRICA; BERBERS, MORISCOS, AND ARABS. RELATIONS WITH MOROCCO WERE DIFFICULT.

THE MEDITERRANEAN WORLD, EUROPEANS AND AFRICANS, HAD A LONG TRADITION OF CAPTIVE AND SLAVE TAKING. THE FAMOUS WRITER MIGUEL DE CERVANTES HIMSELF HAD BEEN A CAPTIVE IN ALGIERS FROM 1575 TO 1580.

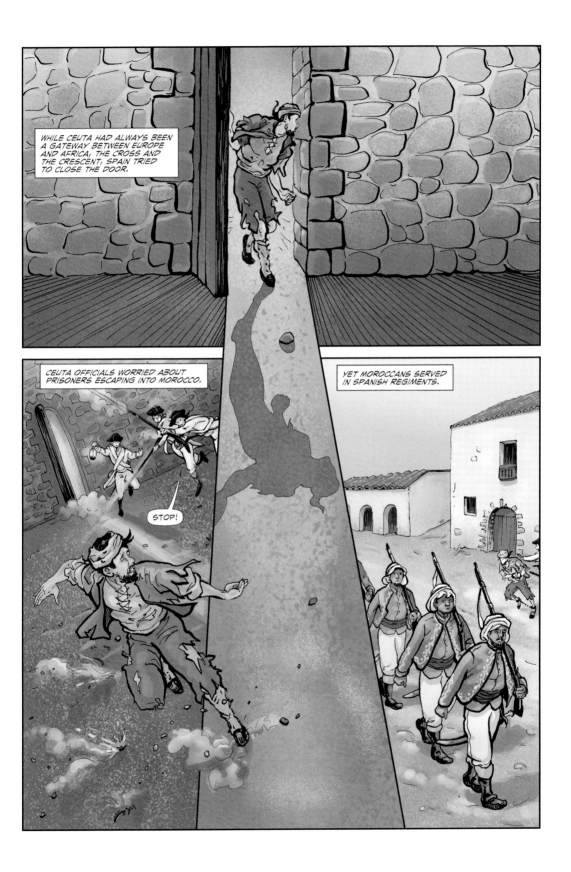

WHILE CEUTA HAD ALWAYS BEEN A GATEWAY BETWEEN EUROPE AND AFRICA, THE CROSS AND THE CRESCENT, SPAIN TRIED TO CLOSE THE DOOR.

CEUTA OFFICIALS WORRIED ABOUT PRISONERS ESCAPING INTO MOROCCO.

STOP!

YET MOROCCANS SERVED IN SPANISH REGIMENTS.

IN DECEMBER 1790, SULTAN MOULAY YAZID OF MOROCCO BEGAN A SIEGE OF CEUTA THAT LASTED INTO 1791.

WATCH OUT!

THE SPANISH USED THEIR CANNONS, ARMED CANOES, AND INCURSIONS TO COUNTERATTACK.

THERE THEY ARE!

IN AUGUST AND SEPTEMBER 1791 MOROCCAN TROOPS ATTACKED THE WALLED CITY, TO NO AVAIL.

THE 1789 FRENCH REVOLUTION SENT SHOCK WAVES ACROSS EUROPE, THE MEDITERRANEAN, AND THE ATLANTIC. CEUTA WAS NO EXCEPTION, PLAYING AN IMPORTANT ROLE IN THE FRENCH REVOLUTIONARY AND NAPOLEONIC WARS (1792-1815).

ALTHOUGH THE SPANISH CROWN PROHIBITED NEWSPAPERS FROM REPORTING ABOUT THE FRENCH REVOLUTION, NEWS SPREAD QUICKLY AND FOREIGN PAPERS CIRCULATED AMONG SOLDIERS AND SAILORS.

THEY WON!

IN 1793 FRANCE DECLARED WAR AGAINST SPAIN, WHICH ALLIED WITH ENGLAND.

CEUTA PROVIDED THOUSANDS OF TROOPS FOR THE WAR OF THE PYRENEES (1793-95). THEY RETURNED WITH NEWS AND STORIES.

THE FRENCH HANGED THE KING!

THEY DECLARED A REPUBLIC.

YET IN 1796 SPAIN ALIGNED WITH THE FRENCH UNDER THE TREATY OF SAN ILDEFONSO. THIS LED TO SPAIN TRANSFERRING LOUISIANA TO THE FRENCH, WHO SOON SOLD IT TO THE UNITED STATES.

His Catholic Majesty having always manifested t the Duke of Parma an aggrandizement, which m with his dignity; and the French Republic having long King of Spain to understand the desire which they fe recover possession of the colony of Louisiana; both gov

CEUTA WAS AN IMPORTANT STAGE FOR NAVY BATTLES. SHIPS RUSHING TO ENCOUNTERS SUCH AS TRAFALGAR, BRITAIN'S CRUSHING DEFEAT OF THE SPANISH AND FRENCH NAVIES IN 1805, PASSED WITHIN SIGHT OF THE PRESIDIO.

IS THAT THE BRITISH?

HUNDREDS OF PRISONERS FROM CEUTA WERE DRAGOONED FOR SHIPS SUCH AS THE SANTÍSIMA TRINIDAD, CONSIDERED THE GREATEST SAILING SHIP OF THE ERA.

DOZENS DIED WHEN IT WAS CAPTURED AND SCUTTLED IN THE BATTLE OF TRAFALGAR.

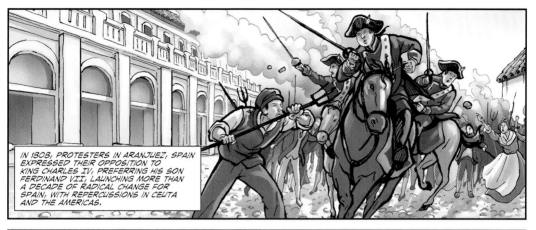

IN 1808, PROTESTERS IN ARANJUEZ, SPAIN EXPRESSED THEIR OPPOSITION TO KING CHARLES IV, PREFERRING HIS SON FERDINAND VII, LAUNCHING MORE THAN A DECADE OF RADICAL CHANGE FOR SPAIN, WITH REPERCUSSIONS IN CEUTA AND THE AMERICAS.

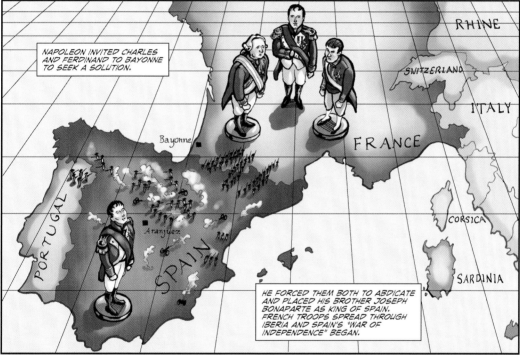

NAPOLEON INVITED CHARLES AND FERDINAND TO BAYONNE TO SEEK A SOLUTION.

HE FORCED THEM BOTH TO ABDICATE AND PLACED HIS BROTHER JOSEPH BONAPARTE AS KING OF SPAIN. FRENCH TROOPS SPREAD THROUGH IBERIA AND SPAIN'S "WAR OF INDEPENDENCE" BEGAN.

VIVA LA JUNTA CENTRAL!

CEUTA JOINED MUCH OF SPAIN IN OPPOSING THE FRENCH OCCUPATION. LIBERALS LED THE RESISTANCE, DEMANDING BROAD CHANGE.

CEUTA HELPED DEFEND THE LIBERAL HOLDOUT, THE PORT OF CÁDIZ. THE NATIONAL ASSEMBLY THERE PASSED A LIBERAL CONSTITUTION IN 1812 THAT OFFERED GREATER RIGHTS FOR SPANISH AMERICA. THESE CHANGES ACCELERATED THE SEARCH FOR REFORM AND INDEPENDENCE FROM MEXICO TO CHILE.

CONSTITUCION politica DE LA MONARQUIA Española. Promulgada en Cádiz a 19. de Marzo de 1812

DEPUTIES FROM ACROSS SPAIN AND THE AMERICAS DEBATED IN CÁDIZ ABOUT VOTING RIGHTS, EQUALITY, AND LIMITS ON THE MONARCHY, THE CHURCH, AND LANDOWNERS. THE LIBERAL MEASURES OFFENDED CONSERVATIVES ON BOTH SIDES OF THE ATLANTIC.

REFEES FLOODED INTO CEUTA, INCLUDING ARISTOCRATS FLEEING THE FRENCH SUCH AS THE DUKE OF MEDINACELI (DON LUIS FERNÁNDEZ DE CÓRDOBA).

PRISONERS ALSO CONTINUED TO ARRIVE. ONE PATRIOT FROM PERU, THE AUGUSTINIAN PRIEST MARCOS DURÁN MARTEL, WOULD RADICALLY CHANGE JUAN BAUTISTA'S LIFE.

64

THE REBELLION SPREAD TO MANY TOWNS BUT SPANIARDS ATTACKED AND ARRESTED DURÁN MARTEL AND OTHER LEADERS IN MARCH.

YOU ARE SENTENCED TO TEN YEARS IN THE ROYAL ARMY.

IN OCTOBER 1812, HE WAS SENT ON THE SAN MIGUEL SHIP FROM CALLAO TO CEUTA TO WORK AT THE HOSPITAL.

CHAPTER 6
FREEDOM

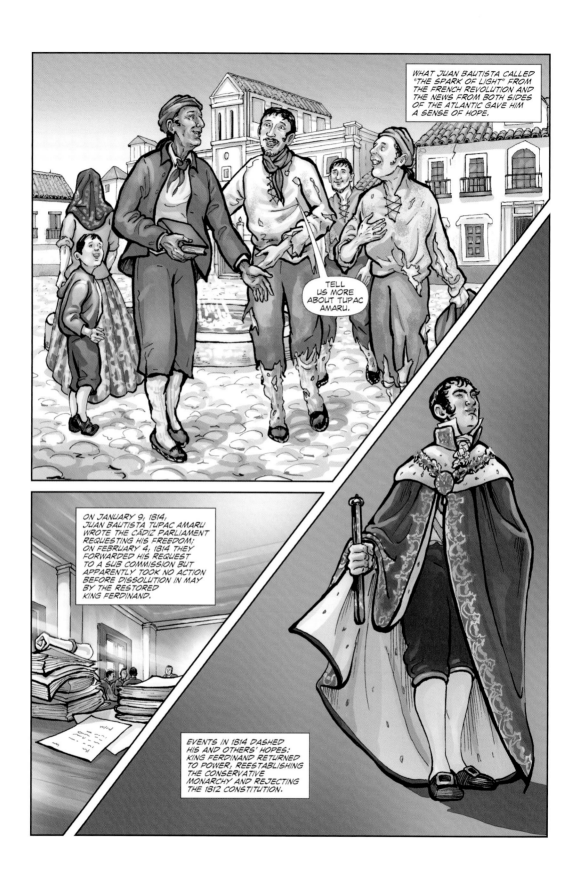

WHAT JUAN BAUTISTA CALLED "THE SPARK OF LIGHT" FROM THE FRENCH REVOLUTION AND THE NEWS FROM BOTH SIDES OF THE ATLANTIC GAVE HIM A SENSE OF HOPE.

TELL US MORE ABOUT TUPAC AMARU.

ON JANUARY 9, 1814, JUAN BAUTISTA TUPAC AMARU WROTE THE CADIZ PARLIAMENT REQUESTING HIS FREEDOM; ON FEBRUARY 4, 1814 THEY FORWARDED HIS REQUEST TO A SUB COMMISSION BUT APPARENTLY TOOK NO ACTION BEFORE DISSOLUTION IN MAY BY THE RESTORED KING FERDINAND.

EVENTS IN 1814 DASHED HIS AND OTHERS' HOPES: KING FERDINAND RETURNED TO POWER, REESTABLISHING THE CONSERVATIVE MONARCHY AND REJECTING THE 1812 CONSTITUTION.

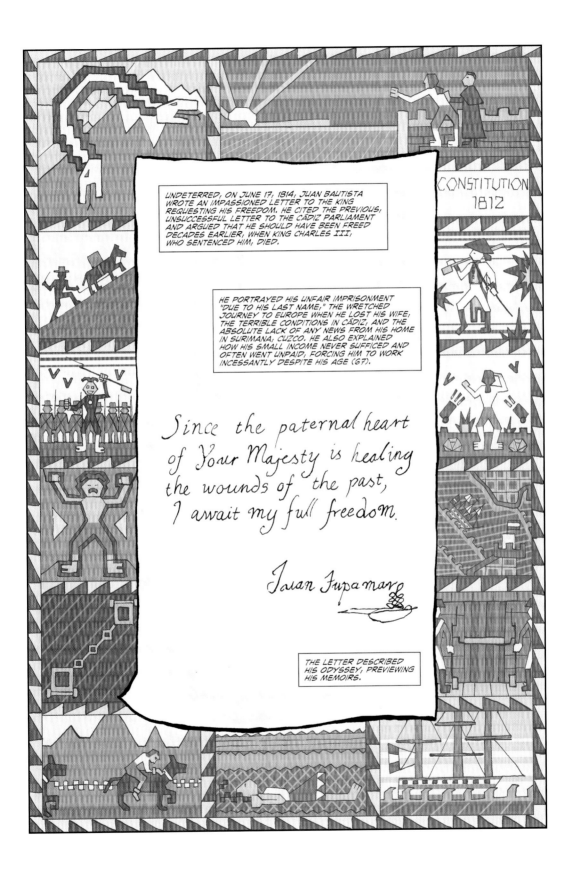

UNDETERRED, ON JUNE 17, 1814, JUAN BAUTISTA WROTE AN IMPASSIONED LETTER TO THE KING REQUESTING HIS FREEDOM. HE CITED THE PREVIOUS, UNSUCCESSFUL LETTER TO THE CÁDIZ PARLIAMENT AND ARGUED THAT HE SHOULD HAVE BEEN FREED DECADES EARLIER, WHEN KING CHARLES III, WHO SENTENCED HIM, DIED.

HE PORTRAYED HIS UNFAIR IMPRISONMENT "DUE TO HIS LAST NAME," THE WRETCHED JOURNEY TO EUROPE WHEN HE LOST HIS WIFE, THE TERRIBLE CONDITIONS IN CÁDIZ, AND THE ABSOLUTE LACK OF ANY NEWS FROM HIS HOME IN SURIMANA, CUZCO. HE ALSO EXPLAINED HOW HIS SMALL INCOME NEVER SUFFICED AND OFTEN WENT UNPAID, FORCING HIM TO WORK INCESSANTLY DESPITE HIS AGE (67).

CONSTITUTION 1812

Since the paternal heart of Your Majesty is healing the wounds of the past, I await my full freedom.

Juan Tupamaro

THE LETTER DESCRIBED HIS ODYSSEY, PREVIEWING HIS MEMOIRS.

WITH THE RETURN OF THE KING AND THE RESTORATION OF THE OLD ORDER, AN INCREASING NUMBER OF PRISONERS REACHED CEUTA, PARTICULARLY SPANISH LIBERALS AND SPANISH-AMERICAN INDEPENDENCE FIGHTERS.

FOUR PROMINENT PRISONERS BEFRIENDED AND AIDED JUAN BAUTISTA:

AGUSTÍN ARGÜELLES, A KEY ARCHITECT OF THE LIBERAL 1812 SPANISH CONSTITUTION...

...FRANCISCO ISNARDI, REVOLUTIONARY LEADER OF VENEZUELA...

...JUAN BAUTISTA AZOPARDO, A MALTESE COMMANDER WHO FOUGHT FOR ARGENTINA...

...AND MARIANO SUBIETA, INDEPENDENCE FIGHTER FROM POTOSÍ (BOLIVIA).

TRAINED AS A LAWYER, ARGÜELLES HAD A PROMINENT ROLE IN CÁDIZ, CALLING FOR LIBERAL MEASURES SUCH AS FREEDOM OF THE PRESS, ABOLITION OF SLAVERY, AND THE FREE MARKET.

WE'LL ALL BE HOME SOON.

IN 1819, A VENEZUELAN OFFICIAL, JUAN ROSCIO, WROTE COLLEAGUES IN LONDON, DEMANDING THE RELEASE OF PRISONERS, INCLUDING JUAN BAUTISTA:

brother of José Gabriel the head of the 1781 insurgency, whose goal was the same as ours, to fight the tyranny of the Spanish government.

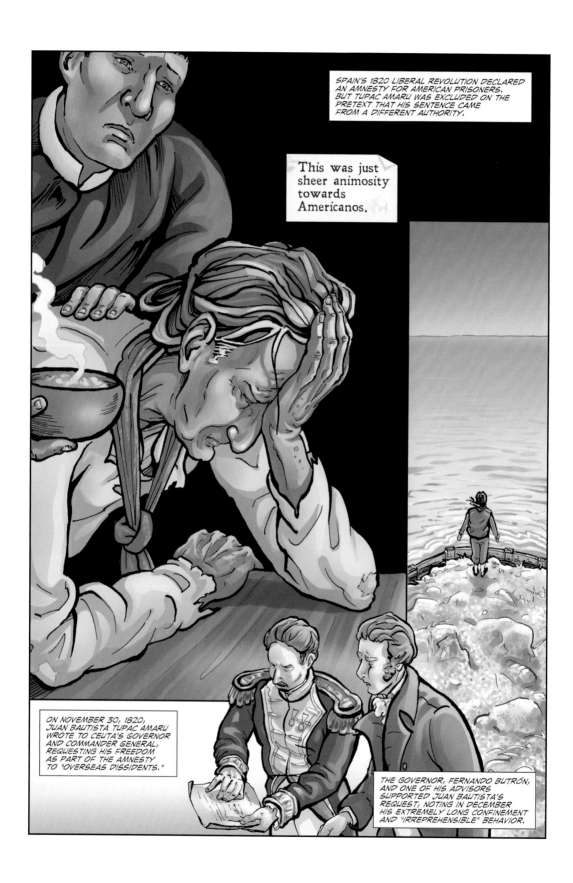

SPAIN'S 1820 LIBERAL REVOLUTION DECLARED AN AMNESTY FOR AMERICAN PRISONERS. BUT TUPAC AMARU WAS EXCLUDED ON THE PRETEXT THAT HIS SENTENCE CAME FROM A DIFFERENT AUTHORITY.

This was just sheer animosity towards Americanos.

ON NOVEMBER 30, 1820, JUAN BAUTISTA TUPAC AMARU WROTE TO CEUTA'S GOVERNOR AND COMMANDER GENERAL, REQUESTING HIS FREEDOM AS PART OF THE AMNESTY TO "OVERSEAS DISSIDENTS."

THE GOVERNOR, FERNANDO BUTRÓN, AND ONE OF HIS ADVISORS SUPPORTED JUAN BAUTISTA'S REQUEST, NOTING IN DECEMBER HIS EXTREMELY LONG CONFINEMENT AND "IRREPREHENSIBLE" BEHAVIOR.

A MADRID NEWSPAPER, EL CETRO CONSTITUCIONAL (THE CONSTITUTIONAL SCEPTER), LAMENTED IN DECEMBER 1820 THAT TUPAC AMARU HAD BEEN dragged from his family and buried for more than 30 years in Ceuta without a sentence besides the will of the King.

IN JANUARY 1821 THE KING APPROVED JUAN BAUTISTA'S REQUEST...

...BUT HE WAS STILL NOT HOME FREE.

ON JANUARY 26 AND 27, 1821, ANOTHER MADRID NEWSPAPER, MISCELÁNEA, RECOUNTED JUAN BAUTISTA'S SAGA AND LAUDED CEUTA'S LIBERALS FOR FREEING HIM AFTER 37 YEARS, an act that will forever echo in the land where he was born.

OTHER LIBERAL PAPERS ALSO TOLD HIS STORY.

DESPERATE, THEY REQUESTED HELP FROM THE NOW POWERFUL AGUSTÍN ARGÜELLES, THE MINISTER OF THE INTERIOR [GOBERNACIÓN] IN THE LIBERAL GOVERNMENT.

HE GOT THEM THE PAPERWORK AND CREDIT THEY NEEDED.

THEY FOUND A SHIP SAILING FOR BUENOS AIRES FROM ALGECIRAS THAT OFFERED THEM AN AFFORDABLE TICKET; ALTHOUGH IN TERRIBLE CONDITIONS.

ON JULY 3, 1822, JUAN BAUTISTA AND HIS DEAR FRIEND FRIAR DURÁN MARTEL BOARDED THE RETRIEVE.

CHAPTER 7
AN INCA KING IN ARGENTINA?

JUAN BAUTISTA AND MARCOS DURÁN MARTEL DIDN'T APPEAR ON THE PASSENGER LIST AND WERE TOLD TO FIND A SPOT ON DECK.

WE DON'T EVEN HAVE COVER.

EXHAUSTED AND EMOTIONAL, JUAN BAUTISTA HAD A BREAKDOWN WHILE WAITING TO SET SAIL. THE CREW WANTED TO SEND HIM ASHORE BUT DURÁN MARTEL WOULDN'T LET THEM.

THE RETRIEVE WAS DELAYED AND DIDN'T HOIST ANCHOR UNTIL AUGUST 3. IT LEFT WITH 12 CREW MEMBERS AND 2 LISTED PASSENGERS (INCLUDING JUAN BAUTISTA'S CEUTA COMRADE AND BOLIVIAN HERO MARIANO SUBIETA).

Algeciras
Ceuta
Canary Islands
North Atlantic Ocean
Equator
South Atlantic Ocean
Buenos Aires
Montevideo

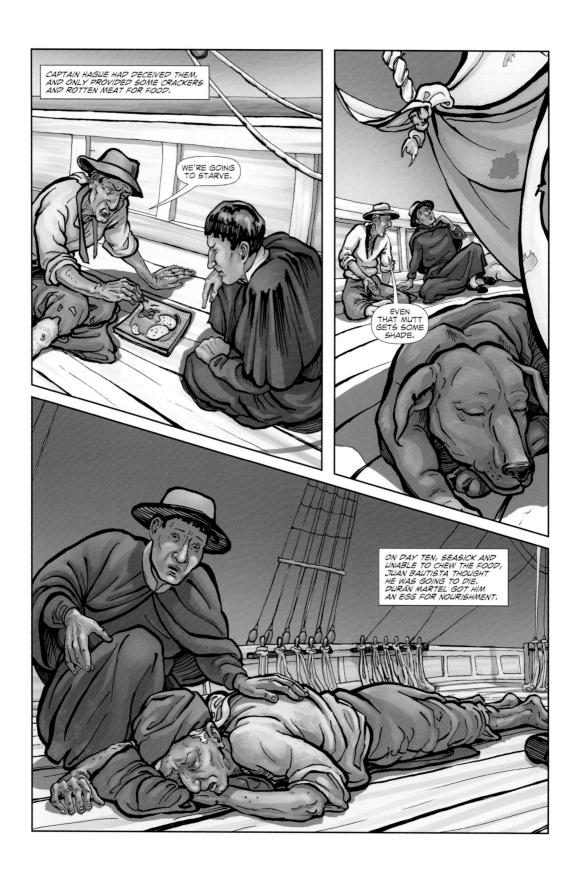

CAPTAIN HAGUE HAD DECEIVED THEM, AND ONLY PROVIDED SOME CRACKERS AND ROTTEN MEAT FOR FOOD.

WE'RE GOING TO STARVE.

EVEN THAT MUTT GETS SOME SHADE.

ON DAY TEN, SEASICK AND UNABLE TO CHEW THE FOOD, JUAN BAUTISTA THOUGHT HE WAS GOING TO DIE. DURÁN MARTEL GOT HIM AN EGG FOR NOURISHMENT.

CAPTAIN HAGUE WAS SO IMPRESSED BY DURÁN MARTEL'S LOVING CARE FOR JUAN BAUTISTA THAT HE ASKED:

WHO IS HE? SOMEONE IMPORTANT?

JUAN BAUTISTA HAD A VERY LOW OPINION OF CAPTAIN HAGUE.

He makes me think that he runs slaves.

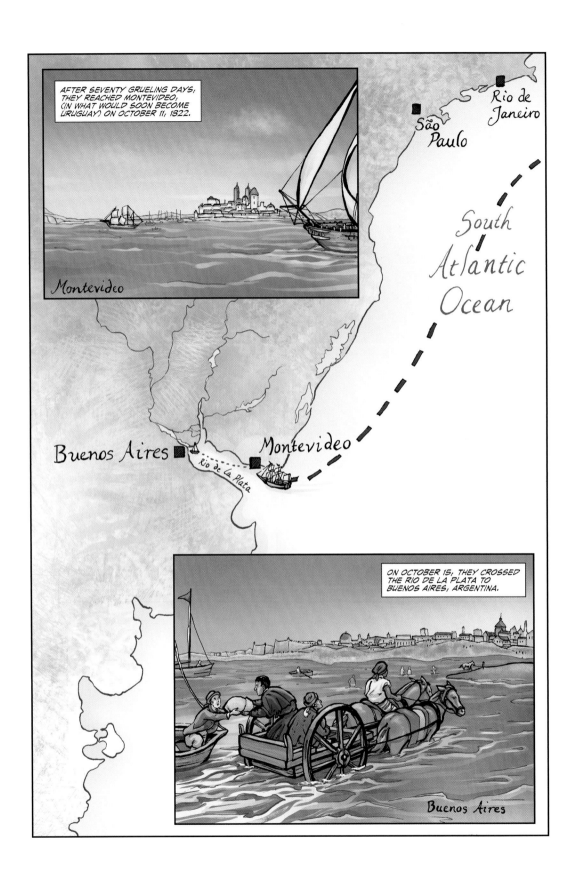

AFTER SEVENTY GRUELING DAYS, THEY REACHED MONTEVIDEO, (IN WHAT WOULD SOON BECOME URUGUAY) ON OCTOBER 11, 1822.

Montevideo

São Paulo

Rio de Janeiro

South Atlantic Ocean

Buenos Aires

Río de la Plata

Montevideo

ON OCTOBER 15, THEY CROSSED THE RÍO DE LA PLATA TO BUENOS AIRES, ARGENTINA.

Buenos Aires

BUENOS AIRES WAS NOT THE COSMOPOLITAN CITY IT IS TODAY, BUT A PORT OF ABOUT 30,000 PEOPLE, OF EUROPEAN, INDIGENOUS, AND AFRICAN DESCENT. IT HAD BECOME THE CAPITAL OF THE NEWLY FORMED RIO DE LA PLATA VICEROYALTY IN 1776.

NEW GRANADA

PERU

BRAZIL

RIO DE LA PLATA VICE ROYALTY

CHILE

Buenos Aires

PATAGONIA

TO HIS GREAT SURPRISE, MANY PEOPLE KNEW WHO JUAN BAUTISTA WAS.

WHY ARE THEY LOOKING AT ME?

THE MALTESE ARGENTINE PATRIOT JUAN BAUTISTA AZOPARDO HOSTED THE TWO RECENT ARRIVALS AS WELL AS THE BOLIVIAN MARIANO SUBIETA.

AZOPARDO AND HIS GUESTS REGALED JUAN BAUTISTA AND DURÁN MARTEL WITH STORIES ABOUT ARGENTINA'S FIGHT FOR INDEPENDENCE.

IN 1806 AND 1807, THE CITY HELPED FIGHT OFF A BRITISH INVASION, RADICALIZING THE POPULATION.

"JUNTAS FORMED IN 1809 IN UPPER PERU, WHAT BECAME BOLIVIA, AND IN BUENOS AIRES IN 1810, THE MAY REVOLUTION. THEY DEMANDED AUTONOMY AND REFUSED TO RECOGNIZE THE FRENCH OCCUPATION OF SPAIN."

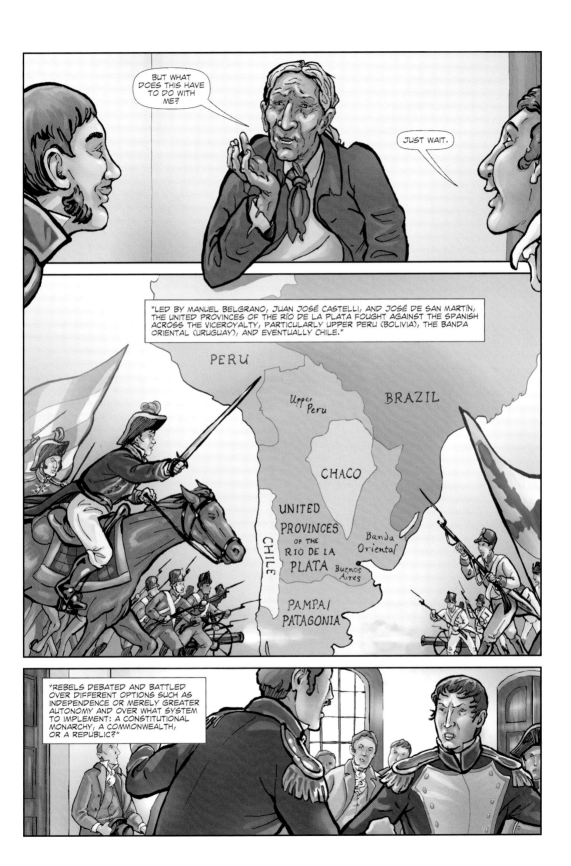

BUT WHAT DOES THIS HAVE TO DO WITH ME?

JUST WAIT.

"LED BY MANUEL BELGRANO, JUAN JOSÉ CASTELLI, AND JOSÉ DE SAN MARTÍN, THE UNITED PROVINCES OF THE RÍO DE LA PLATA FOUGHT AGAINST THE SPANISH ACROSS THE VICEROYALTY, PARTICULARLY UPPER PERU (BOLIVIA), THE BANDA ORIENTAL (URUGUAY), AND EVENTUALLY CHILE."

PERU

Upper Peru

BRAZIL

CHACO

UNITED PROVINCES OF THE RÍO DE LA PLATA

CHILE

Banda Oriental

Buenos Aires

PAMPA! PATAGONIA

"REBELS DEBATED AND BATTLED OVER DIFFERENT OPTIONS SUCH AS INDEPENDENCE OR MERELY GREATER AUTONOMY AND OVER WHAT SYSTEM TO IMPLEMENT: A CONSTITUTIONAL MONARCHY, A COMMONWEALTH, OR A REPUBLIC?"

INFLUENCED BY ROMANTIC VISIONS OF THE INCAN EMPIRE, BELGRANO AND OTHERS BELIEVED THE INCA KING PROPOSAL COULD GAIN INDIGENOUS SUPPORTERS IN THE ANDES AND WOULD STAVE OFF OPPOSITION IN EUROPE FROM THE CONSERVATIVE HOLY ALLIANCE FORMED BY RUSSIA, AUSTRIA, AND PRUSSIA IN THE WAKE OF NAPOLEON'S DEFEAT IN 1815. THE ALLIANCE PREFERRED ANY TYPE OF MONARCHY OVER A REPUBLIC.

ACTA
DE INDEPENDENCIA
DECLARADA POR EL CONGRESO DE LAS PROVINCIAS-UNIDAS
EN SUD-AMERICA.

VERSION PARAFRASTICA EN IDIOMA
AYMARA.

ARGENTINA'S DECLARATION OF INDEPENDENCE ("UNITED PROVINCES OF SOUTH AMERICA") WAS PRINTED IN QUECHUA AND AYMARA AND AN INCA SUN APPEARED PROMINENTLY ON ITS FLAG AND COINS.

CRITICS RIDICULED THE IDEA OF AN INCA KING, DERIDING MONARCHISM AND ALSO THE IDEA OF AN INDIGENOUS LEADER:

"A monarchy in sandals"

"A King with dirty feet"

"A King taken from a shack"

89

JUAN BAUTISTA ARRIVED TO A BUENOS AIRES UNDERGOING AN INCA CULTURAL BOOM, INCLUDING BOOKS AND PLAYS ABOUT HIS BROTHER.

IN 1816, A BOOK APPEARED ABOUT JOSÉ GABRIEL'S DEATH AND A NEWSPAPER PUBLISHED HIS 1781 DEATH SENTENCE.

IN 1821, A FIVE-ACT PLAY "TUPAC AMARU" WAS STAGED, TO CELEBRATE THE REBELLION.

IN 1822, WITH ARGENTINA STILL NOT UNIFIED, BERNARDINO RIVADAVIA SERVED AS THE MINISTER OF GOVERNMENT OF BUENOS AIRES.

ON OCTOBER 22, 1822, JUAN BAUTISTA WROTE RIVADAVIA, SUMMARIZING HIS HARDSHIPS AND REQUESTING

a place to live and some aid for my upkeep, until providence allows me to return to my native country.

RIVADAVIA ANSWERED TWO DAYS LATER, ORDERING THAT THE GENERAL MEN'S HOSPITAL GIVE JUAN BAUTISTA ROOM AND BOARD AND ASSIGNING HIM A PENSION OF 30 PESOS A MONTH FOR THE LENGTH OF HIS STAY IN BUENOS AIRES.

EL ARGOS DE BUENOS AIRES (#81, OCTOBER 26, 1822) ANNOUNCED THIS DECISION; NOTING THAT IT WAS "ON THE CONDITION THAT HE WRITE UP IN HIS OWN HAND THE TEXT HE SHOWED TO THE GOVERNMENT THAT DESCRIBED HIS SUFFERINGS." THIS INDICATES THAT HE HAD A DRAFT OF HIS MEMOIRS.

JUAN BAUTISTA AND DURÁN MARTEL LIVED IN THE GENERAL MEN'S HOSPITAL.

THE ONLY TRACE OF DURÁN MARTEL WE HAVE IS IN AN 1824 MEMOIR OF THE IRISH SURGEON JOHN OUGHGAN THAT INCLUDES A DOCUMENT FROM MARCOS DURAND MARTEL (SIC); "CHAPLAIN OF THE HOSPITAL."

Del Señor Capellan del Hospital, Marcos Martel El Capellan de este hospital general de hombres

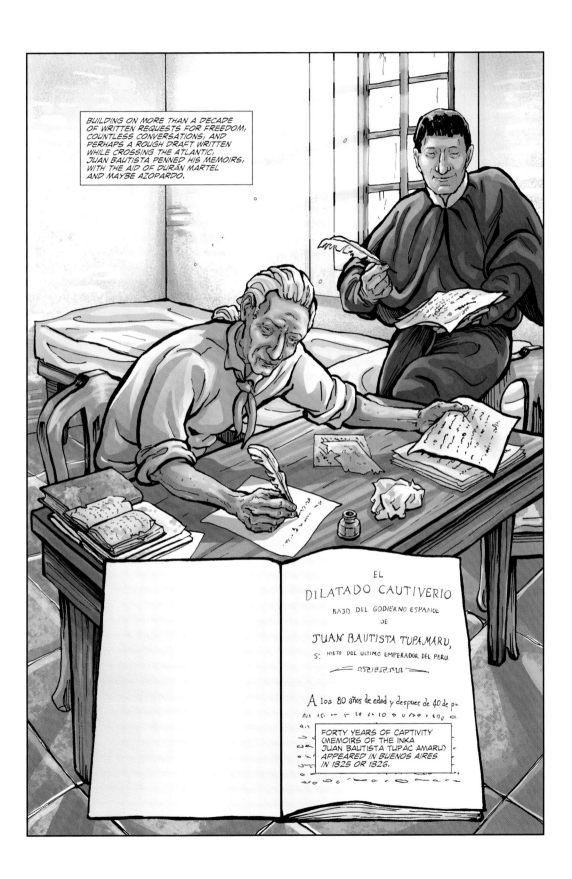

JUAN BAUTISTA DID NOT GIVE UP HOPE OF RETURNING TO PERU. ON MAY 15, 1825, HE WROTE THE LIBERATOR SIMÓN BOLÍVAR, WHO WAS IN CUZCO. AFTER SUMMARIZING HIS HARDSHIPS, HE IMPLORED

I still hold in my heart the pleasant hope of breathing the air of my homeland [patria], and I am confident that the great Bolívar will attend this request, in light of his large and generous soul....if I could just see my Liberator, and with this consolation enter my grave.

HE DID NOT RECEIVE A RESPONSE.

94

JUAN BAUTISTA DIED
IN BUENOS AIRES ON
SEPTEMBER 2, 1827,
AT THE AGE OF EIGHTY.
(HIS DEATH CERTIFICATE
HAS NOT BEEN FOUND.)

HE WAS BURIED IN AN UNMARKED PLOT
SOMEWHERE IN THE RECENTLY INAUGURATED
LA RECOLETA CEMETERY IN BUENOS AIRES.

THE FINAL PARAGRAPH OF HIS MEMOIRS LAUDED DURÁN MARTEL.

All the glory and much more goes to him ... . He brought me back to life

THEY ENDED

with the hope that these memoirs make people think about how to prevent tyranny, which proved in my case to be so abominable.

HE DIED WITH THE SATISFACTION OF BEING A FREED MAN BUT THE FRUSTRATION OF NOT RETURNING TO HIS NATIVE LAND.

WE KNOW NOTHING ABOUT THE FATE OF FRIAR DURÁN MARTEL, JUAN BAUTISTA'S FAITHFUL FRIEND AND SOUL MATE.

CHAPTER 8

JUAN BAUTISTA: A FORGOTTEN HERO

THE BROTHER OF THE LEADER OF THE LARGEST REBELLION IN COLONIAL SPANISH AMERICAN HISTORY AND A PARTICIPANT IN THE UPRISING ITSELF; A VICTIM OF NEARLY FORTY YEARS OF HARSH IMPRISONMENT ON BOTH SIDES OF THE ATLANTIC; A POTENTIAL INCA KING; AND THE AUTHOR OF STUNNING MEMOIRS OF HIS TRAGIC LIFE— JUAN BAUTISTA HAD ALL THE ELEMENTS TO BECOME A NATIONAL HERO IN PERU AND AN INTERNATIONAL SYMBOL.

SHOCKINGLY, HE WAS LARGELY FORGOTTEN UNTIL THE MIDDLE OF THE TWENTIETH CENTURY AND IS STILL NOT WIDELY KNOWN.

LOS PEQUEÑOS GRANDES LIBROS
DE HISTORIA AMERICANA

Serie 1   Tomo 1

CUARENTA AÑOS DE CAUTIVERIO

(Memorias del Inka Juan Bautista Tupac Amaru)

IN 1941, HOWEVER, A PERUVIAN HISTORIAN,
FRANCISCO LOAYZA, PUBLISHED
JUAN BAUTISTA'S MEMOIRS ALONG WITH
IMPORTANT DOCUMENTATION FROM THE
ARCHIVO DE INDIAS IN SEVILLE ABOUT HIM.

ARCHIVO
GENERAL
DE
INDIAS

FROM 1934-36, LOAYZA AND HIS DAUGHTER
MARÍA EMILIA LOAYZA REVIEWED AND PHOTOGRAPHED
THOUSANDS OF DOCUMENTS IN SPAIN,
JUST BEFORE THE ONSET OF THE SPANISH CIVIL WAR.
LOAYZA WAS THE PERUVIAN CONSUL.

Despite the fact that the
author is Peruvian, these
memoirs are not found in
Peru's National Library
and remain completely
unknown in Peru.

FRANCISCO LOAYZA, "INTRODUCTION," 1941, 13-14

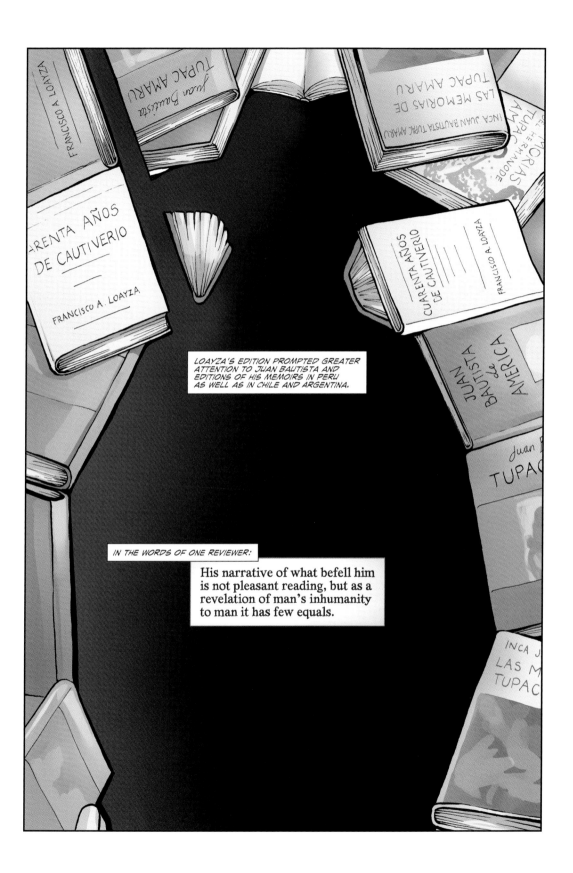

LOAYZA'S EDITION PROMPTED GREATER
ATTENTION TO JUAN BAUTISTA AND
EDITIONS OF HIS MEMOIRS IN PERU
AS WELL AS IN CHILE AND ARGENTINA.

IN THE WORDS OF ONE REVIEWER:

His narrative of what befell him
is not pleasant reading, but as a
revelation of man's inhumanity
to man it has few equals.

IN CUZCO, A WALL WITH JUAN BAUTISTA'S NAME
LOOMS LARGE IN THE TUPAC AMARU PLAZA
WHILE A PLAQUE ON A MOUND IN THE MUNICIPALITY
MARKS THE SITE WHERE DIRT FROM THE RECOLETA
CEMETERY WAS PLACED IN HIS HONOR IN 1973.

BUT THERE IS STILL MUCH TO BE LEARNED ABOUT JUAN BAUTISTA TUPAC AMARU.

HE REMAINS IN AN UNMARKED GRAVE IN BUENOS AIRES AND HAS RECEIVED LITTLE RECOGNITION IN PERU, ARGENTINA, OR ELSEWHERE.

PART II
HISTORICAL CONTEXT

EPIC

1: *a long narrative poem in elevated style recounting the deeds of a legendary or historical hero*
   • *the* Iliad *and the* Odyssey *are epics*
2: *a work of art (such as a novel or drama) that resembles or suggests an epic*
3: *a series of events or body of legend or tradition thought to form the proper subject of an epic*

Juan Bautista Tupac Amaru's memoirs, *Cuarenta años de cautiverio* or *Forty Years of Captivity*, have all the essentials of an epic. It tells a tale so riveting and stark that many deemed it fiction, a story too extreme to possibly be true. They were, however, legitimate memoirs penned by Juan Bautista. While not a poem in the style of Homer's *Iliad* and *Odyssey*, they have a blunt, direct style that captivates the reader, using as a foundation rich details and brief but powerful laments about his travails. Juan Bautista's life was filled with more tragedies than triumphs and had a bittersweet ending; he found freedom when he was nearly eighty years old, but never returned to his native Peru.[1]

This introduction addresses some of the mysteries about his saga, explains how we know what we know, and advances certain arguments about Juan Bautista's life. In doing so, it explores a few topics that many scholars have gotten wrong, from conditions in Ceuta to the fundamental question of whether he was the author of the memoirs. It also explains why Juan Bautista was a "witness to the Age of Revolutions"—how he rubbed shoulders with a fascinating transatlantic cast of characters in the period stretching from the French Revolution to Spanish American independence. His story is an

---

[1]   I am using his first names rather than Tupac Amaru to avoid confusion with his famous brother and other family members. All translations throughout the book are mine unless otherwise noted.

entryway into the revolts and revolutions that rocked both sides of the Atlantic from the 1780s to the 1820s.

JUAN BAUTISTA TUPAC AMARU AND THE ANDEAN UPRISINGS

Juan Bautista Tupac Amaru was born in 1747 in Tungasuca, south of the former Inca capital, Cuzco. His father was Miguel Condorcanqui Usquionsa Tupac Amaru, a prominent muleteer and *kuraka*, the ethnic authorities that represented Andean communities under Spanish colonialism. He was a direct descendent of Tupac Amaru, the last Inca ruler, beheaded by Viceroy Toledo in 1572. His mother was Ventura Monjarrás. Both were of mixed descent, indigenous and Spanish, but had strong ties to local indigenous culture; spoke Quechua, the language of the Incas; and belonged to an *ayllu* (Callco), an indigenous social unit and neighborhood.[2] Juan Bautista had a famous half-brother, José Gabriel Condorcanqui, Tupac Amaru II, the leader of the largest uprising in colonial Spanish America. José Gabriel was born in 1738 and his mother, Rosa Noguera, died three years later, in 1741. Both brothers participated at a young age in the family's muleteer business, overseeing the shipment of goods on mules from Cuzco to the silver mines of Potosí and into what became northern Argentina. Their father passed away in 1750, so Juan Bautista was raised largely by his mother, Monjarrás. Documents from the era refer to José Gabriel playing with and looking after his little brother.[3]

Juan Bautista's life cannot be understood outside that of his more famous brother. In October 1780, José Gabriel (hereafter called Tupac Amaru, a name he used to underline his royal Inca blood) and his wife, Micaela Bastidas, imprisoned a Spanish authority, the *corregidor* Antonio de Arriaga, and announced an end to abusive treatment of the indigenous population, roughly 60 percent of the Viceroyalty of Peru and a higher percentage in the Cuzco area.[4] The rebels hanged Arriaga several days later in a public ceremony in which Tupac Amaru denounced in Quechua the Spanish tyranny in front of

---

[2]   Carlos Daniel Valcárcel, *La familia del Cacique Túpac Amaru (documentos existentes en la Iglesia de Pamapamarca)*, 2nd ed. (Lima: UNMSM, 1979), 45–46.

[3]   Testimonies by José Sánchez and Mónica Sánchez, *Colección Documental del Bicentenario de la Revolución Emancipadora de Túpac Amaru*, "Los procesos a Túpac Amaru y sus compañeros," IV, 2 (Lima: CDBRETA, 1982), 619–621. The literature on the Tupac Amaru Rebellion is vast. For two recent overviews, see Sergio Serulnikov, *Revolution in the Andes: The Age of Túpac Amaru* (Durham, NC: Duke University Press, 2013); Charles F. Walker, *The Tupac Amaru Rebellion* (Cambridge, MA: The Belknap Press of Harvard University Press, 2014).

[4]   Carlos Contreras and Marcos Cueto, *Historia del Perú contemporáneo* (Lima: Red para el Desarrollo de las Ciencias Sociales en el Perú, 1999), 33.

thousands of indigenous peasants. In the following months they recruited followers, hunted down Spanish authorities, and sacked haciendas and textile mills, particularly those owned by Europeans. The rebels presented an ambiguous platform, claiming to fight in the name of the king of Spain and to respect all non-Europeans, while waging a ferocious guerrilla war and calling for a return of the Incas or at least Inca justice. They built on Inca revivalism, the belief that Inca rule was superior to that of the Spanish; traditional notions of colonial rule or "good government"; and certain elements of the Enlightenment. The rebels were searching for a model—keep in mind that the United States was in the midst of establishing itself as an independent nation, while the French and Haitian Revolutions had yet to take place.

The rebellion spread rapidly in the Cuzco region and allied itself with a series of uprisings led by the Kataristas to the south, in the area that became Bolivia. Colonial authorities in Lima rapidly learned that they were facing much more than a local revolt, common in the period. At the end of 1780, they sent thousands of troops from Lima, the bulk of them mulattos and other dragooned soldiers. In April 1781, these forces captured Tupac Amaru, Micaela Bastidas, and much of their inner circle, executing them in a grisly public ritual on May 18. However, three men continued the struggle: Diego Cristóbal Tupac Amaru, Juan Bautista and Tupac Amaru's cousin; Andrés Mendigure, a relative of Micaela Bastidas; and Tupac Amaru and Bastidas's son, Mariano Tupac Amaru. Shockingly young (26, 18, and 17), these leaders of the second phase redirected the uprising to the south, toward Lake Titicaca and the Katarista rebels. The rebellion became even more violent, as neither side took prisoners and both committed atrocities. The rebels had the upper hand, yet surprisingly accepted a ceasefire in early 1782, when they were on the verge of victory. Months later, Royalists falsely claimed that the rebels had not complied with the terms of the agreement and, in 1783, arrested the rebel leaders, executing them in brutal fashion. The largest rebellion in Spanish American colonial history had ended, with over a hundred thousand dead. Both the victors and the defeated understood that Spanish rule had hung in the balance.[5]

Juan Bautista did not have a leadership role in the rebellion. All of the testimonies cast him as an aide to his brother and nothing more. For example, a Spanish witness insisted that Juan Bautista never touched a gun or commanded soldiers.[6] Tupac Amaru might not have had great confidence in his younger brother, or perhaps he was trying to protect him. Juan Bautista's diminished

---

[5]   Serulnikov, *Revolution*; Walker, *The Tupac Amaru Rebellion*.

[6]   Testimony by Diego Ortigoza, *Colección Documental del Bicentenario de la Revolución Emancipadora de Túpac Amaru*, "Los procesos a Túpac Amaru y sus compañeros," IV, 2, 610.

role ultimately saved him from a death sentence. A small group led by a local authority arrested Juan Bautista a few days after the May 18 execution of his brother, sister-in-law, and other rebels. They found him hiding in a small canyon in a ravine between Surimana and Tungasuca, along with his wife Susana Aguirre and his mother. He had among his possessions a bag with 134 pesos (a considerable sum that his captors assumed that he "must have stolen"), a satchel with gunpowder and bullets, and two small paintings, one of Our Lady of Carmen and the other the royal seal of Castilla and León. His captors kept fourteen pesos as a reward.[7] He was accused of carrying his brother's bed during the first phase of the rebellion, serving as his aide-de-camp, and participating in battles such as that of Paucartambo, to the northeast of Cuzco.

In the trial, he identified himself as Juan Tupamaro (he only occasionally used his middle name, while his last name was spelled in multiple ways over the years), thirty-four years old, a farmer and muleteer from Tungasuca, married to Susana Aguirre, identified as a Spaniard. We know little about her. He claimed that he was not actually Tupac Amaru's brother, as he had been born before Ventura Monjarrás married Miguel Tupac Amaru. He also contended that he had had a minor role in the uprising and that he was coerced. Testimonies from local people who knew him refuted his denial. The eighty-year old Joseph Sánchez, "an old and sick man," remembered Juan Bautista's baptism and called him the spitting image of his father.[8] Juan Bautista could not sign his document. In light of his brother's excellent education, it is surprising that he was illiterate at this point. It might have been a ruse to highlight his naiveté and insignificance in a vast uprising.[9]

Guards took Juan Bautista in chains to Cuzco, where prosecutors sought the death penalty for his role in the rebellion and for being Tupac Amaru's brother. They also wondered if the portrait of Saint Carmen broke the rules of the Inquisition due to its "bad quality." He was sentenced to two hundred lashes in a public ceremony and exile to San Juan de Ulúa, the prison fortress in Veracruz, Mexico. Nonetheless, he remained in jail in Cuzco. In his

[7] His trial is found in Archivo General de Indias, Cuzco, Legajo 32. For a reliable transcription, see *Colección Documental del Bicentenario de la Revolución Emancipadora de Tupac Amaru*, "Los procesos a Tupac Amaru y sus compañeros" (Lima: Comisión Nacional del Bicentenario de la Rebelión Emancipadora de Tupac Amaru, 1982, tomo IV, II), 607–631. The "stolen" quote is from p. 607. For more valuable documents, see *Colección Documental de la Independencia del Perú*, esp. tomo 2, vol. 3, *La rebelión de Tupac Amaru*, ed. and introduced by Carlos Daniel Valcárcel (Lima: Comisión Nacional del Sesquicentenario de la Independencia del Perú, 1971), hereafter CDIP.

[8] *Colección Documental del Bicentenario de la Revolución Emancipadora de Tupac Amaru*, "Los procesos," 619–620.

[9] Walker, *The Tupac Amaru Rebellion*, 18–19.

memoirs, he described physical abuse such as a guard jamming his pinkie into the trigger guard of a musket and squeezing it until he bled, as well as a filthy, overcrowded cell with hostile prisoners and appalling, insufficient food. He claimed he and his fellow inmates were given rancid meat discarded in the local market, and that the warden encouraged the guards to beat him. In addition, he and other chained prisoners were paraded around Cuzco on mules, for public ridicule.[10] To Juan Bautista's great surprise, he was freed in early 1782, his release a by-product of the ceasefire negotiations. The time in jail had taken a physical toll, and he and Susana Aguirre hobbled while returning to Pampamarca. Those loyal to the Spanish taunted them. Once at home, Juan Bautista noted that those who supported the Spanish mistreated them, while those who had supported the rebellion wondered if he could have done more.

In 1783, the hardliners who had taken control among Spanish authorities deemed the ceasefire an error, claiming that the rebels had broken the agreement by fostering dissent and subversion. They arrested the three young leaders of the rebellion's second phase, Andrés Mendigure and Mariano Tupac Amaru in Lima on February 26 and Diego Cristóbal in Tungasuca on March 14. They sentenced the leaders to death for not respecting the pardon and acting in bad faith. In a ghastly public ritual on July 19 in Cuzco's Regocijo Plaza, Diego Cristóbal had to witness the execution of allies and family members, including his mother. Executioners then tore his skin off with burning hot pincers, dragged him to the gallows, and hanged him. They quartered him and displayed his body parts across the Cuzco region.

Spanish authorities prosecuted many more rebels in 1783 than two years earlier, including virtually anyone related to the Tupac Amaru family. Indeed, they were explicit about getting rid of the entire family. The trials ultimately found about half of the accused innocent but sentenced seven people to death (those executed on July 19), banished or exiled from Peru twelve, and sent sixty-one Tupac Amaru family members to Lima, where their fate would be decided. Juan Bautista and Susana Aguirre were part of this latter contingent. In March 1783 a local authority or *corregidor* had invited him to lunch and seized him, sending him to prison in Cuzco. A priest in Pomacanchi oversaw the burning of his house and the salting of his fields. Juan Bautista was surprised that he was not among those executed in July; over the following forty years, there would be many dire moments when he would wish they had done so.

On October 6, 1783, after seven months of hunger and abuse in jail, he, Susana Aguirre, and seventy-six other prisoners left for Lima accompanied by a hundred guards. Sixty-one of them were Tupac Amaru relatives, including Juan Bautista's uncle, who Juan Bautista claimed was 125 years old. Susana

---

[10]   Francisco Loayza, ed., *Cuarenta años de cautiverio (Memorias del Inka Juan Bautista Túpac Amaru)* (Lima: Lib. e Imp. D. Miranda, 1941), 26–29.

Aguirre's father, Ventura Aguirre; sister, Nicolasa; and brother-in-law An-tolín Ortíz were also among the chained prisoners. The contingent included seventeen children (ranging in age from four months to nine years); thirty-five women, most of them elderly; and twenty-six men, including one in his eighties.[11]

It is at this point where Juan Bautista's memoirs pick up in pace and tension. He aptly uses the word "odyssey" to describe the following five years. Guards shackled the prisoners' hands and feet and led them around the main plaza in Cuzco. While many jeered the prisoners, one kind soul gave Juan Bautista a horse, which would greatly improve conditions on the journey. Other prisoners rode broken-down mules, many of which died, a sign of extremely tough conditions. They crossed the Andes, including peaks over 13,000 feet above sea level. Juan Bautista describes incessant cruelty by the guards toward the thirsty, hungry, and exhausted prisoners. He watched his mother die of dehydration, when the guards paid no attention to her desperate pleas for water.[12] The contingent lost their way near Castrovirreyna, among the breathtakingly high mountain passes between Huamanga and the coast, and ran out of water; soldiers had to break through ice to find a muddy puddle. Once on the coast, the prisoners had to bear the relentless sun and chilly evenings in the desert that runs from Ica to Lima, finally trudging into Lima on November 22, 1783. Six had died on the journey and one had escaped.[13] Guards deposited them in dungeon-like cells in the San Felipe Fort in Callao. Juan Bautista was likely placed in a dark semicircular passage, so narrow that prisoners could only lie down sideways. The prisoners were chained to one another and Juan Bautista describes feeling his comrades shake from malaria and watching them die, including his uncle. Guards never unshackled them and the filth became unbearable[14]

EUROPE, AFRICA, AND THE AGE OF REVOLUTIONS

In March 1784 the Lima High Court (Audiencia) sentenced Juan Bautista and several other Tupac Amaru family members to ten years of hard labor in a Spanish presidio. After delays due to Spain's war with England, two warships left Callao for Spain on April 13, 1784, the *San Pedro de Alcántara* and *El*

---

[11]   CDIP, II, 3, 392-393.

[12]   Her death certificate can be found at CDIP, II, 3, 424.

[13]   CDIP, II, 3, has many documents related to this journey, particularly 390–429. See also Walker, *The Tupac Amaru Rebellion*, 249–256.

[14]   I thank Officer Christian Rodríguez Aldana for a tour of San Felipe Fort. I suffered extreme claustrophobia within five minutes of entering the cell where Juan Bautista was probably held. Loayza, *Cuarenta años*, 36–37.

Peruano, both dangerously overloaded with gold, silver, and copper. Juan Bautista, Susana Aguirre, and Mariano (Tupac Amaru and Micaela Bastidas's son) boarded *El Peruano*, along with twenty-six other prisoners. The trip was horrific. Juan Bautista describes hunger; illnesses such as rampant scurvy; no protection from the elements except a ragged poncho and a sheepskin, even during a snowstorm near Cape Horn; and constant abuse by the crew. The prisoners remained on deck, tethered to one another. His wife, Susana Aguirre, died on the night of April 20, one week after departure. In all likelihood, she was ill when she boarded. Juan Bautista lay attached to his dead wife until the next morning, when crew members dumped her body into the Pacific Ocean. In his memoirs, Juan Bautista wrote that those who love their spouses would understand "how I wanted to die at that moment."[15] French scientist Joseph Dombey was among the ship's free passengers. In his memoirs he provides details about the trip, including the rudder breaking and how he paid crew members to dive into the freezing ocean to fix it. He never mentions the prisoners.[16]

Mariano died while the *El Peruano* crossed Cape Horn and was unceremoniously heaved into the Atlantic. As noted in the graphic history, Juan Bautista spent four miserable months tied to the mast in dock in Rio de Janeiro while the ship's rudder was fixed. The misery continued during the Atlantic crossing, when crewmembers played a practical joke on him and he broke some ribs. He also complained that the Spanish would not allow the prisoners to pray. *El Peruano* reached Cádiz on March 1, 1784; only eleven of the prisoners who left Lima had survived. Seven of them would die in Cádiz in the next four years. Juan Bautista was so weak that guards had to carry him to his cell. Nonetheless, they added a twenty-five-pound weight to his chains. The other ship carrying the Peruvian prisoners, the *Alcántara*, had a worse fate. It wrecked near Peniche, Portugal and eighteen prisoners died. The Spanish claimed to have lost 7.5 million pesos in precious metal. They contracted divers to recover what they could.[17] These passages from Juan Bautista's memoirs tell one horror story after another.

Juan Bautista complained about his miserable quarters in the San Sebastián castle—a dark, humid room with almost no light and only a sheepskin and some rags as bedding. He lamented that no Spanish guard showed any

---

[15] Loayza, *Cuarenta años*, 39. Diego Cristóbal's wife, Manuela Tito Condori, had died in a Callao hospital weeks before the ships departed. Eulogio Zudaire, *Agustín de Jáuregui, virrey del Perú* (Pamplona, Spain: Diputación Foral de Navarra, Dirección de Turismo, Bibliotecas y Cultura Popular, 1971), 446.

[16] "Historical Account of Jos. Dombey, Translated from the French of M. Deleuze (Concluded)," *The Belfast Monthly Magazine* 2, no. 7 (February 28, 1809): 120–126. For a list of the prisoners who died in route, see CDIP, II, 3, 427–428 (reproduced in the Primary Sources section).

[17] The prisoners who had reached Cádiz on *El Peruano* had to wait for sentencing because their trial records were on the *Alcántara*. CDIP II, 3, p. 459, May 9, 1785.

humanity towards him; the Swiss Guard treated him better. After three years, he was sentenced to Ceuta, a Spanish presidio (garrison or fort) located in northern Africa, just across from Gibraltar.[18]

Spain's Northern African presidios (Ceuta, Melilla, Orán, Alhucemas, and Peñón de Vélez de la Gomera) had become increasingly important for eighteenth-century Spain as a means to hold prisoners and to defend the Mediterranean. Unlike the British penal colony of Australia or those of the French in Guiana and New Caledonia that consisted of convicts and a small population of guards, the Spanish presidios combined prisoners, a free population, and a strong armed presence, all under military management. Reflecting the utilitarian notions of the era, they put the prisoners to work, reinforcing the forts' walls, preparing ships, and producing war supplies. In times of conflict, the prisoners would serve on the ships or at the front lines. In this era, over half of Spain's convicts did their time in one of these, most sentenced between six and the maximum of ten years. Juan Bautista, however, ended up confined for more than thirty.[19]

Biographers have misunderstood Juan Bautista's decades in Ceuta. In light of these misinterpretations and my own unfamiliarity with the region, much of my research focused on Ceuta, including an enlightening visit. Many writers have used the term *mazmorras* or dungeons to describe his dwelling there. However, he was actually part of the free population, a *confinado* allowed to circulate and not forced to work. When arriving in chains from Ceuta, the pilot separated him from the common prisoners and told the Ceuta governor and count of Las Lomas, Don Miguel Porcel y Manrique de Arana, that Juan Bautista was not the same as the other ruffians and deserved better conditions. The governor instructed his assistant to place him in a private home.[20] This, however, did not signify freedom or economic stability. He stayed with a silversmith who exploited him terribly, working him relentlessly and barely offering enough food. Juan Bautista received a small pension but had to work on the side to have enough to survive. But this arrangement was

---

[18]   He was granted a daily pension of six reales (3/4 of a peso), which proved to be barely sufficient for his upkeep. CDIP II, 3, p. 467, Cádiz, April 26, 1788.

[19]   Ruth Pike, *Penal Servitude in Early Modern Spain* (Madison: University of Wisconsin Press, 1983); Christian De Vito, "The Spanish Empire: 1500–1998," in *A Global History of Convicts and Penal Colonies*, ed. Clare Anderson (London: Bloomsbury Academic, 2018), 65–95; Jose Miguel Palop-Ramon, "Delitos y penas en la España del siglo XVIII," *Estudis: Revista de Historia Moderna* 22 (1996): 65–105, which provides data on the sentencing; Antonio Carmona Portillo, *Ceuta, Melilla y Tánger: 8 artículos y un documento inéditos*. Málaga: np, 2019, esp. chapter 5.

[20]   The vast majority of prisoners in Ceuta were common prisoners; Palop-Ramón, "Delitos."

far better than living in a vile cell in the Hacho prison amongst dangerous prisoners and hostile guards.

Life was not easy for Juan Bautista in Ceuta. The presidio had a population of about ten thousand, split almost evenly among the civil population, prisoners, and the military. A slim peninsula with the Atlantic Ocean on the one side and the Mediterranean Sea on the other, Ceuta then and now served both as an entry point and bulwark against Morocco.[21] He lived through the siege of 1790–1791, when Sultan Moulay Yazid bombarded the peninsula almost daily and Spanish forces counterattacked on land and with canoes and boats. Currently, barbed-wire fences protect the border, passed every day by tens of thousands of Moroccans who work in Ceuta as well as by tourists and authorities heading in and out of Morocco.

Juan Bautista complained in his memoirs about his treatment by the silversmith and his wife, and at some point in the 1790s he moved out, to a dwelling in what is now downtown Ceuta. He grew food and presumably worked odd jobs. Documents from 1812, 1818, and 1819 show him as living on Calle Real (or right off it, on San Simón), on what is today Santiago Coriat Street.[22] These documents refer to him as "don," a show of respect, and spell his name variously as Tupac Amaru, Tupa Camaro, and Tupacamaru. In another rare appearance in the archival record, he served as a witness in a domestic abuse case. He and a friend, Josef Escudero, were having dinner when they heard shouts. They learned that a man named Tornero was hitting his wife. Juan Bautista, Escudero, and others rushed to their room but it was locked; Tornero burst out of the room in his underwear. His wife had several wounds that she confirmed were inflicted by her husband. Juan Bautista signed his testimony with a lovely signature, proof of his literacy.[23]

In several sections of his memoirs, Juan Bautista mentions his weak Spanish and lack of writing skills. In the Cuzco trials from the 1780s, he denied his kinship with Tupac Amaru, a ploy that prosecutors did not take seriously, and also stressed his naiveté and lack of education. In his memoirs he noted that his efforts to educate himself in Ceuta were received with "scorn and mockery." In the same paragraph, he describes his decision to move out of the

---

[21] Residents in Ceuta pointed out to me the different color of the water on the north, the Atlantic, and the South, the Mediterranean. Some might disagree with this distinction and instead prefer the geographical name Strait of Gibraltar.

[22] In 1819, Don Juan Tupac Amaro is listed as living with Marcos Martel; in 1818 as Juan Tupacamaro; and in 1812 as Don Juan Tupa Camaro. The documents from 1812 and 1819 are from Archivo Parroquial de Nuestra Señora de los Remedios. Padrones Parroquiales, Ceuta. I thank the distinguished historians Antonio Carmona for these and Dr. José Luis Gómez Barceló for the 1818 document.

[23] Archivo General de Ceuta, Fondo Carlos Posac Mon, Legajo 30. José Luis Gómez Barceló shared this and other documents with me. One curiosity: Juan Bautista states his age as thirty-seven—impossible, as he reached Ceuta in 1788 at the age of forty or forty-one.

"Don Juan tupa Camaro" (eleventh from top) registered as living independently just off Calle Real (San Simón) in 1812. Archivo Parroquial de Nuestra Señora de los Remedios. Padrones Parroquiales. Año 1812, Ceuta.

"Don Juan Tupacamaro" (fourth from top) registered as living on San Simón in 1818. The cross indicates that he had confessed and taken communion in Lent. Archivo Parroquial de Nuestra Señora de los Remedios. Padrones Parroquiales. Año 1818, Ceuta.

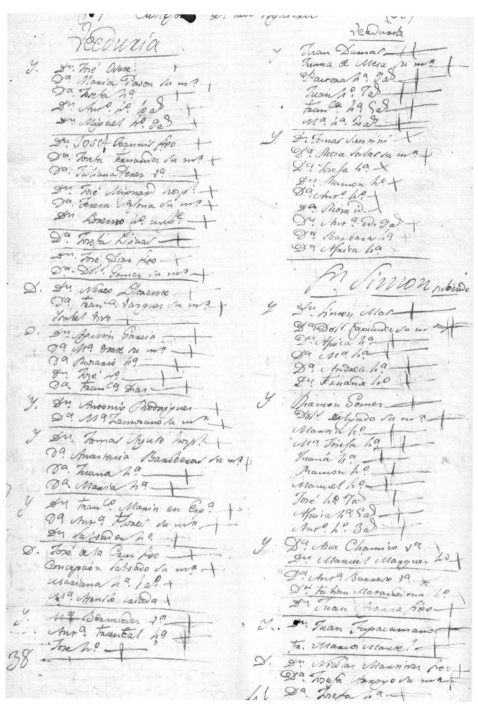

1819, "Don Juan Tupacamaro" and "Friar Marcos Martel" (fourth and fifth from bottom right) registered as living together on San Simón, 1819. Archivo Parroquial de Nuestra Señora de los Remedios. Padrones Parroquiales. Año 1819, Ceuta.

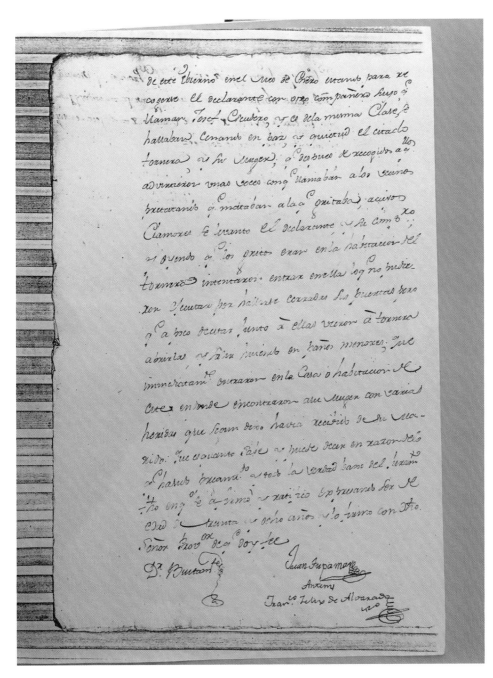

"Juan Tupamaro" signature from undated testimony about domestic abuse that he witnessed. The signature indicates his literacy. The document gives his age as thirty-eight, impossible as he reached Ceuta in his forties. Archivo General de Ceuta, Fondo Carlos Posac Mon, Legajo 30, fotocopia de documento manuscrito de procedencia desconocida.

silversmith's house. He understood educating himself and gaining independence as one and the same.[24] I believe that he had some education in Peru and greatly improved his writing skills while in Ceuta. He had plenty of time to learn and others would have aided him. It is likely that his guardian angel, Friar Marcos Durán Martel, tutored him.

A mestizo (combined indigenous and European descent) from the Huánuco area of Peru who had previously worked as a carpenter, and whose family had property, Durán Martel joined the Augustinian order as a young man. He became involved in a violent uprising against the Spanish in Huánuco in 1812. As was the case in Mexico with fathers Miguel Hidalgo and José Manuel Morelos, some members of the Catholic Church played important roles in the rebellions and conspiracies taking place across Spanish America in the early nineteenth century. They opposed the Crown's efforts to squeeze the Church of revenues and power and joined others who contested social injustices and crushing taxes. Huánuco was a violent mass uprising in which creoles (people of European descent born in the Americas) and Indians first fought separately and then allied to take several towns, killing Spaniards and ransacking estates and stores. Spanish measures that threatened the region's main crop, tobacco, helped spark the insurgency. Durán Martel initially conspired from his monastery and penned letters that called for Indians to collect any weapons they could find and join the rebels. Documents refer to him as the "Captain of the Indian rebels" and "the head of this Insurgency," but also describe his ability to stay out of the spotlight. Witnesses used terms such as "shadowy" and "elusive"; Ella Dunbar Temple, in an important document collection published in 1971, called him "dour."[25] One witness claimed that he heard Durán Martel declare that Spaniards (*Chapetones*) should be punished "because they harass creoles, hitting and mistreating whenever they want, and only came to Huánuco to make money."[26] The uprising spread quickly but collapsed when the Spanish sent well-armed troops from Lima. Durán Martel eluded capture for two months but was ultimately arrested by Spanish forces.

---

[24] Loayza makes this same point in a footnote; *Cuarenta años*, 50.

[25] Ella Dunbar Temple, ed., "Prólogo," in *Conspiraciones y rebeliones en el siglo XIX. La Revolución de Huánuco, Panataguas y Huamalíes. Colección Documental de la Independencia del Perú* 1 (III) (Lima: Comisión Nacional del Sesquicentenario de la Independencia del Perú, 1971, I–XCVII); quotes from pp. 58 and 59. This is an excellent introduction to this mass uprising. See also F. Javier Campos y Fernández de Sevilla, "Presencia de los agustinos en la revolución peruana de Huánuco," *Anuario Jurídico y Económico Escurialense* XLV (2012): 637–686, 639 for the "head" quote.

[26] Quote from CDIP III, 2, 237; Marissa Kelly Bazán Díaz, "La rebelión de los sectores populares en la rebelión de Huánuco, 1812: saqueadores, seductores e incanistas" (master's thesis, History Department, Universidad Nacional Mayor de San Marcos, 2017), 34.

Prosecutors shielded Durán Martel from the death sentence other leaders received, but still exiled him to Spain. He reached Ceuta in June 1813, and in 1814 wrote a bitter memorandum about his tough conditions and his work at the Ceuta Hospital.[27] He and Juan Bautista became extremely close, roommates who were inseparable until the latter's death. The 1818 Ceuta census record indicates that they lived together. It seems very likely that in their free time they would have improved Juan Bautista's reading and writing skills. Durán Martel was well educated. For his priestly training, he would have taken a minimum of three years of philosophy and four of theology. In his memoirs, Juan Bautista makes many classical references. These might have come from Durán Martel's teachings or from the friar's collaboration.[28]

Skeptics about the memoirs point to Juan Bautista's illiteracy and also the timing—he produced them very rapidly once in Buenos Aires. But my research has shown that with the support of Durán Martel, Juan Bautista wrote numerous requests for freedom and memos that told his story. I believe these ultimately served as first drafts for his memoirs. On January 9, 1814, Juan Bautista wrote to the Cádiz Parliament requesting his freedom. They forwarded his letter to a subcommission, but took no action before the Parliament's dissolution in May. Juan Bautista persisted and wrote King Ferdinand VII on June 17, 1814, pleading to be pardoned and released. He explained that he had played no role in his brother's uprising and that his sentence to a presidio in Spain had been illegal, contrary to the Laws of the Indies, the body of laws overseeing Spanish colonialism. He mentioned the death of his wife Susana Aguirre on the journey to Spain, stressing that he had no children to look after him. He used the same timeline as his memoirs, written a decade later.[29] These impassioned requests and petitions served as rough drafts for his memoirs. Furthermore, as Francisco Loayza pointed out in 1941, the information from the memoirs harmonize with the detailed information from the 1781–1783 trials, which had not been made public. Only Juan Bautista could describe in the early 1820s his relationship with his family, his role during the rebellion, and his capture with details that matched perfectly the

---

27 Archivo de Indias, LIMA, Leg. 1015 s/n. letter from Fray Marcos Durán Martel to Crown, July 8, 1814, from Ceuta (reproduced in the Primary Sources section).

28 I thank Father Javier Campos y Fernández de Sevilla for his help on many questions about Durán Martel, including his education.

29 Archivo General de Indias, Indiferente, Legajo 1351. I thank Luis Miguel Glave for providing me this rich document. The literature on Cádiz is massive. One valuable set of essays is Scott Eastman and Natalia Sobrevilla Perea, *The Rise of Constitutional Government in the Iberian Atlantic World. The Impact of the Cádiz Constitution of 1812* (Tuscaloosa: University of Alabama Press, 2015); see especially Sobrevilla Perea, "Loyalism and Liberalism in Peru, 1810–1824," 111–132, therein. Also important is Víctor Peralta Ruíz, *En defensa de la autoridad. Política y cultura bajo el gobierno de Virrey Abascal, Perú 1806–1816* (Madrid: Consejo Superior de Investigaciones Científicas, 2002).

testimonies of people who knew and captured him four decades earlier. He was the author of the memoirs, likely aided by Durán Martel.[30]

This brings us to Juan Bautista's growing political consciousness, his role as a "witness to the Atlantic Revolutions." In his memoirs, Juan Bautista noted how his confidence in the victory of the "kingdom of reason" kept his spirits up in the toughest times. He explained that in his old age, once in Argentina, he appreciated how "human spirit marches enlightened against the Crown."[31] In fact, in the first paragraph of his memoirs, he sustains that his unjust imprisonment and decades of horrors "would have remained hidden among so many others, suffocated by the powers that be, if the universal conflagration with which humanity is making their monarchs tremble had not weakened the Crown in Spain."[32] Juan Bautista declared that he owed his freedom to the Enlightenment and global antimonarchical forces.

Ceuta helps explain his understanding of the Age of Revolutions. This slim northern African peninsula housed hundreds of political prisoners in the thirty-five years that Juan Bautista spent there, decades that spanned the French Revolution and Spain's Liberal Revolution. He befriended numerous prisoners from Spanish America, such as Mariano Subieta from Bolivia, Juan Bautista Azopardo from Malta and Argentina, and Francisco Isnardi from Venezuela. He also hobnobbed with Agustín Argüelles, who became a leading Liberal in Spain. These prisoners instructed Juan Bautista and Durán Martel about the struggles for autonomy and independence in Spanish America, the Napoleonic invasion of Iberia, and the Liberal-led fight against the French. All of them would play decisive roles in Juan Bautista's struggle for freedom. He also had daily contact with a long list of prisoners and malcontents of different political stripes, who were presumably eager to while away the long prison hours hearing his amazing tale of the Tupac Amaru Rebellion and sharing their own experiences and insights. Moreover, Ceuta was an important military center, supplying the Spanish navy for important Mediterranean battles such as Trafalgar in 1805 and serving as the base of operations for Spain's thorny relations with neighboring Morocco. Sailors and soldiers passed along news and rumors, circumventing Spanish censorship about the French and Haitian Revolutions. They brought along tattered newspapers in a variety of languages, discussing their content out loud.

Political discontent escalated in these decades, the apex of the Age of Revolutions. In his memoirs, Juan Bautista lauded the United States: "In the north of our hemisphere a nation that had been a slave like mine broke its

---

[30]   Loayza, *Cuarenta años*, 93, who points out the congruence between the memoirs and Hilario Yañez's testimony.

[31]   Loayza, *Cuarenta años*, 25.

[32]   Loayza, *Cuarenta años*, 15–16.

chains to create institutions that support virtue."[33] The United States had declared its independence in 1776, just four years before the Tupac Amaru Rebellion.[34] He referred to the French Revolution as a "spark of light." He described how he had grown increasingly confident about the struggle for independence in Spanish America because of the "arrival of many prisoners due to this struggle, the oppression faced by *Americanos*, and the harsh echoes from all of Europe that reached the presidio every day."[35] Juan Bautista met political prisoners and veterans who fought in Spain's numerous wars across the globe. He learned about events in France, Haiti, Spanish America (including his native Cuzco), and elsewhere, while changes in Spain itself gave him renewed hope for freedom.

In 1808 Napoleon invaded Iberia, replacing King Charles IV (who was vying for power with his son Ferdinand) with his brother Joseph Bonaparte. This triggered a series of reactions and transformations that altered Juan Bautista's path to freedom. With the army in disarray, Spain's main governing body, the Junta Central, took refuge in the south. Spanish Liberals led a national resistance, based in the Cádiz Cortes or Parliament, which had as its main task the creation of a new constitution. Needing allies, the Liberals invited representatives from Spanish America to participate. This sparked deep debate about who had the right to vote. If elections included people of indigenous and African descent, the *Americanos* would vastly outnumber the Spanish. The great challenge for the Cádiz Cortes was how to replace the Ancien Régime, a hereditary monarchy, with a liberal nation while maintaining Spain's American and Philippine holdings. Many dissidents in Spanish America did not trust the promise of equality and continued to push for secession from Spain. The confinement of the King and the creation of the Cádiz Constitution prompted a sovereignty crisis throughout Spanish America.[36]

Juan Bautista directed his request for freedom in 1814 to Cádiz. While sympathetic to Spanish American political prisoners, the Cortes did not convert the Tupac Amaru Rebellion into a symbol, a precursor. Perhaps the uprising was too violent and radical; it had also occurred three decades earlier, before the global impact of the French Revolution and its many aftershocks. Furthermore, the Cortes was struggling to survive and implement its liberal policies. It faced the opposition of the French forces and Spanish monarchists

---

[33]   Loayza, *Cuarenta años*, 25.

[34]   The United States did not serve as an important model, it seems, for Tupac Amaru. The Spanish censored news from the North and the British still had the upper hand in the late 1770s.

[35]   Loayza, *Cuarenta años*, 54–55.

[36]   Josep M. Fradera, "Include and Rule: The Limits of Liberal Colonial Policy, 1810–1837," in *Connections after Colonialism: Europe and Latin America in the 1820s*, eds. Matthew Brown and Gabriel Paquette (Tuscaloosa: University of Alabama Press, 2013), 65.

as well as various political responses across the Atlantic, from loyalism to the king to radical secession.[37] As it happened, Ferdinand assumed power in 1814, reversing Liberal policies implemented in his father's absence and filling Ceuta with prisoners from the Americas and Spain sympathetic to Juan Bautista's plight. However, a military uprising in January 1820 brought the Liberals back into power, which they held until 1823.

It was during the beginning phases of "the Liberal Triennium" that Durán Martel and Juan Bautista shared their story with the sympathetic press. They correctly insisted that Juan Bautista's experience of over three decades of imprisonment was cruel and unique. Other political prisoners were released much quicker, especially in the early nineteenth century with frequent regime changes. No other Spanish American prisoner had spent so long in Spanish confinement. In 1820 and 1821, *El Cetro Constitucional* (Madrid), *Miscelánea* (Madrid), *Diario Constitucional* (Barcelona), and the *Tertulia Patriótica* (Isla de León) told his dramatic story, from the Tupac Amaru Rebellion to his three decades in Ceuta.[38] Providing the information for these stories no doubt made the task of writing the memoirs a few years later much easier.

HOME?

Juan Bautista's release from Ceuta was not simple, and the impediments and delays must have been particularly frustrating for a man in his seventies. When Liberals took power in 1820, they freed many prisoners, but Juan Bautista was not on the list: so few prisoners remained who had been sentenced by King Charles III (who ruled from 1759–1788) that they were not included. Also, Peru remained a Spanish stronghold, so unlike Azopardo or Isnardi, who received support for their efforts to return from the nascent countries of Argentina and Venezuela, Juan Bautista did not have advocates in Peru. Durán Martel was released before Juan Bautista, but would not cross the Atlantic without his soul mate. They not only had trouble finding the money

---

[37] Scarlett O'Phelan Godoy and Georges Lomné, eds., *Voces americanas en las Cortes de Cádiz: 1810–1814* (Lima: Instituto Francés de Estudios Andinos, Pontificia Universidad Católica del Perú, 2014); Fradera, "Include and Rule"; Gabriel Paquette, *The European Seaborne Empire: From the Thirty Years War to the Age of Revolutions* (New Haven, CT: Yale University Press, 2019), esp. 190–206.

[38] *El Cetro Constitucional, Seminario Político* (Madrid), #1, December 1820, 22–23; *Miscelánea de Comercio, Política, y Literatura* (Madrid), #333, January 26, 1821, 4, and January 27, 1821, #334, 2–3; *Diario Constitucional, Político y Mercantil de Barcelona*, Barcelona, #37, February 6, 1821, 1–2 (reproduced in the Primary Sources section). This last paper refers to a text on Juan Bautista in the *Tertulia Patriótica de la Isla de León*, but I could not find a copy of this Cádiz newspaper.

to pay for the trip (worsened by some problems with Isnardi) and encountered numerous bureaucratic delays, but when Juan Bautista was released from Ceuta, he fell down some stairs and broke his arm. They finally boarded the *Retrieve* on July 3, 1822.

Juan Bautista was not certain he would survive the crossing of the Atlantic.[39] Distraught over more than a month-long delay in departing and the terrible conditions aboard the ship (he glumly noted in his memoirs that a mutt had a better spot on the deck), he had a nervous breakdown before they set sail.[40] His plight brings to mind Mediterranean refugees two centuries later, those fleeing Syria and Africa, battered yet determined to reach freedom.

It took the *Retrieve* seventy days to reach Montevideo and from there Juan Bautista and Durán Martel took a smaller ship across the Rio de la Plata to Buenos Aires. Argentina was a work in progress, still not a unified nation and divided not only about who belonged and the extension of its borders, but also about what type of political system to implement. In the coming years, Uruguay would become an independent country, while the pampas and the northwest became integral parts of Argentina. Juan Bautista and Durán Martel arrived in 1822 in the waning moments of an influential wave of Inca nationalism. In 1816, with the declaration of Argentina's independence in the Congress of Tucumán, the leader of the independence forces, Manuel Belgrano, had sought a constitutional monarchy, with an Inca descendent as head of state. The Argentine flag and its currency displayed Inca suns, and in the early 1820s, Buenos Aires witnessed the publication of books and plays about the Incas; the press also lauded the Tupac Amaru Rebellion. Belgrano died in 1820 but the fascination with the Incas lingered. At least for those who had been followers of Belgrano, Juan Bautista arrived as an unexpected hero.[41]

---

[39] It is at this point in his memoirs, in 1822, that he refers to himself as eighty-four years old. In an 1825 letter to Bolívar he refers to himself as eighty-six, and he uses the term "octogenarian" in several documents. This would mean he was born around 1738 or 1739. In his 1781 trial, however, he confirms that he was born in 1747 and that he was Tupac Amaru's younger brother (Tupac Amaru was born in 1738). A birth year of 1747 seems correct, and the references to being an octogenarian must have been a mistake or an exaggeration.

[40] Marcel Velásquez Castro believes that it might have been epilepsy. Marcel Velásquez Castro, "El cautiverio de la memoria. Voces y subtextos en un autodocumento (1825) de Juan Bautista Túpac Amaru," in *Autobiografía del Perú republicano. Ensayos sobre historia y la narrativa del yo*, eds. Ulrich Mücke and Marcel Velázquez (Lima: Biblioteca Nacional del Perú, 2015), 45–65, 48.

[41] Gabriel Di Meglio, *1816: La verdadera trama de la independencia* (Buenos Aires: Planeta, 2016); Jesús Díaz Caballero, "Incaísmo as the First Guiding Fiction in the Emergence of the Creole Nation in the Provinces of Río de la Plata," *Journal of Latin American Cultural Studies* 17, no. 1 (2008): 1–22; Bartolomé Mitre, *Historia de Belgrano y de la independencia argentina* (Buenos Aires: F. Lajouane, 1887).

Juan Bautista and Durán Martel stayed with their friend from Ceuta, the Argentine Maltese naval hero Azopardo.[42] On October 22, 1822, Juan Bautista petitioned Bernardino Rivadavia, the minister of government of Buenos Aires (Argentina had not yet unified), for help, "a place to live and aid for his upkeep" until he could return to Peru. Rivadavia responded affirmatively two days later, providing them room and board in the General Hospital, on the condition that Juan Bautista write his memoirs in "his own handwriting."[43] The rapidity of Rivadavia's response hints that the arrangement might have been discussed previously or even prearranged. Scholars disagree about the meaning of "his own handwriting." Those who doubt that Juan Bautista wrote the memoirs believe this stipulation was a warning not to invent or plagiarize, while those more sympathetic to him believe it was a demand that he hand in either a neater or more developed version of the preliminary summary that he provided Rivadavia. I am inclined to believe the latter—they were requesting that he develop his autobiography.[44] *El Dilatado Cautiverio bajo del Gobierno Español de Juan Bautista Tupamaru, 5 nieto del Último Emperador del Perú* (*The Dilated Captivity under the Spanish Government of Juan Bautista Tupamara, 5th Generation Descendent of the Last Emperor of Peru*) was published in Buenos Aires sometime between 1824 and 1826.[45]

His memoirs told the story of his "odyssey," his decades in jails and presidios in Peru, Spain, and Africa. They serve as the base of this graphic history. They are rabidly anti-Spanish, a reflection of both Tupac Amaru's suffering and the rhetoric of the era. He wrote them in Buenos Aires, the site of anticolonial wars that had lasted for over a decade and that in 1822 and 1823 continued in Peru and what became Bolivia. Some critics contend that the anti-Spanish rhetoric indicates that the memoirs were more political propaganda than memoir and perhaps written by someone other than Juan Bautista. However, if anyone had grounds to despise the Spanish it was Juan Bautista. Moreover, the vivid details show that Juan Bautista wrote them; even his occasional errors with dates and minor facts help confirm that they were written by a man in his late seventies who might recall some events from

---

[42] On Azopardo, see Mercedes G. Azopardo, *Coronel de Marina Juan Bautista Azopardo* (Buenos Aires: Secretaria de Estado de Marina, 1961).

[43] See translations of these documents in the Primary Sources section.

[44] Juan Canter, "El raro folleto de un impostor," *Boletín del Instituto de Investigaciones Históricas*," Buenos Aires, tomo XIII, March 1935; Loayza refutes Canter's argument that Juan Bautista could not possibly have written the memoirs. Loayza, *Cuarenta años*, 78–83; see also Eduardo Astesano, *Juan Bautista de América: El Rey Inca de Manuel Belgrano* (Buenos Aires: Ediciones Castañeda, 1979), 185–186.

[45] The year of publication is unclear. Astesano says 1824; the Biblioteca Nacional of Peru puts it at 1826. Astesano, *Juan Bautista*, 186.

nearly half a century earlier with a detail or two wrong.[46] It is very likely that Durán Martel aided him; Azopardo could have done so as well.[47]

In light of Juan Bautista's Inca lineage, his blood ties to the Tupac Amaru Rebellion, his sprawling story that stretches from his native Peru to Rio de Janeiro, Cádiz, Ceuta, and Buenos Aires, and his suffering and persistence, it would seem logical that he would have become a well-known historic figure in Peru and even Argentina and his memories be deemed part of the national literary canon. Both countries had just defeated the Spanish (who in 1823 still occupied much of Peru's central Andes, the region where Juan Bautista had watched his mother die) and, like any nascent nation, needed heroes and a useable past. But this was not the case.

Why? The changing political winds in Argentina and Peru and some bad or ill-intentioned reviews that deemed the memoirs a fake prevented Juan Bautista from becoming a national symbol. In Argentina the power of the Belgrano forces faded in the 1820s, particularly with the rise of Juan Manuel de Rosas, who became governor of Buenos Aires in 1829 and had a long political career as an anti-federalist authoritarian. Rosas and his ideologues had no interest in the Incas and ridiculed the notion of a Quechua-speaking monarch. In post-independence Peru, conservatives and liberals alternated in power, but neither side developed the notion that the Peruvian nation evolved from the Incas or underscored the importance of the Tupac Amaru Rebellion. In the decades after independence in 1821, some intellectuals and politicians mentioned Tupac Amaru, but he in no way became part of the national pantheon of heroes. Many people in Lima and beyond associated him with Indian subversion, Cuzco federalism, or even caste war, all projects they abhorred. He did not become an official national hero until 1968 and Juan Velasco Alvarado's "Revolutionary Government of the Armed Forces."[48] Velasco implemented leftist policies and employed Tupac Amaru as his government's key symbol.

As it happened, a single review damaged the reputation of *Forty Years of Captivity* and of Juan Bautista himself. In 1836, Pedro de Angelis lauded the

---

[46]   Loayza notes that not only had forty years passed between the Tupac Amaru uprising and the writing of the memoirs, but that Juan Bautista had not witnessed the execution of his brother and other events he describes. Small factual errors were thus almost inevitable. Loayza, *Cuarenta años*, 22.

[47]   Velásquez Castro, Astesano, and Faverón Patriau show that Durán Martel most likely collaborated. Velásquez Castro, "El cautiverio," 62; Astesano, *Juan Bautista*, 185–186; Gustavo Faverón Patriau, *Contra la alegoría: hegemonía y disidencia en la literatura latinoamericana del siglo XIX* (Hildesheim: George Olms Verlag, 2011), chapter 2, 73–93.

[48]   On the historical memory of Tupac Amaru, see Cecilia Méndez, "La historia hay que reescribirla todita," *Ideele* (Lima) 229 (May 2013); Charles Walker, "The General and His Rebel: Tupac Amaru and the Velasco Revolution," in *The Peculiar Revolution: Rethinking the Peruvian Experiment under Military Rule*, eds. Carlos Aguirre and Paulo Drinot (Austin: University of Texas Press, 2017), 49–72.

Tupac Amaru Rebellion but called Juan Bautista "an impostor" and his memoirs "apocryphal." A native of Naples, Angelis had been invited to Argentina by the Liberal-leaning Bernardino Rivadavia to edit newspapers and promote cultural activities. He switched allegiances to the conservative Rosas and became one of his key ideologues. In 1836, Angelis published a five-volume document collection, including an invaluable set of documents on the Tupac Amaru Rebellion where he passed judgment on the memoirs.[49] The eminent English geographer and historian Clements Markham as well as many others repeated Angelis's assessment, declaring, "It is now confidently asserted that the author of this pamphlet was an impostor."[50] Angelis's evaluation pushed Juan Bautista and his memoirs toward obscurity.

A few nineteenth-century scholars and newspapers mentioned the memoirs, debating their veracity. For example, in his 1875 biography of Simón Bolívar, Felipe Arrazábal deemed Juan Bautista a "venerable martyr."[51] In 1880, the *Opinión Nacional de Caracas* and the *Estrella de Panamá* and the *Daily Star and Herald* reproduced a letter Juan Bautista wrote to Bolívar.[52] Juan Bautista appeared sporadically and randomly in a variety of nineteenth-century publications. A series of journalistic articles in Argentina one hundred years after Juan Bautista's death, however, rekindled the debate about his memoirs and likely inspired Francisco Loayza.

In 1927, the Argentine weekly *Caras y Caretas* published a note sympathetic to Juan Bautista, written by "Aristippus." The text chronicled Juan Bautista's tragic life and concluded glumly that in contemporary Argentina, this refugee would not have been quickly granted a pension but instead subjected to endless bureaucratic delay.[53] Three years later, the Argentine poet and tango composer Héctor Pedro Blomberg wrote a compassionate summary of Juan Bautista's tale based on his reading of the memoirs in the National Library. Blomberg compared *Forty Years* to Dumas's *The Count of Monte Cristo* and the 1830s prison memoirs of the Italian patriot Silvio Pellico. Readers will indeed find intriguing parallels between Juan Bautista and the bitter count, Edmond Dontès. Argentine intellectuals in this period

---

[49]   Pedro de Angelis, "Discurso preliminar a la revolución de Tupac Amaru," in his *Colección de obras y documentos relativos a la historia antigua y moderna de las provincias de Río de la Plata* (Buenos Aires: Imprenta del Estado, 1836, tomo V). See especially pp. vii–viii.

[50]   Clements R. Markham, *Travels in Peru and India While Superintending the Collection of Chinchona Plants and Seeds in South America, and Their Introduction into India* (London: John Murray, Albemarle Street, 1862), 168.

[51]   Felipe Larrazábal, "La vida de Bolívar," In *Correspondencia del General del Libertador Simón Bolivar* (New York: Edward Jenkins, 1875, tomo 1), 141.

[52]   *Estrella de Panamá*, November 25, 1880 (32, 427), p. 1; *The Daily Star and Herald*, November 19, 1880; it reproduces the text from the Caracas newspaper.

[53]   Aristippus, "A los 85 años, pobre y enfermo, llegó a Buenos Aires un hermano del Inca Tupac-Amaru," *Caras y Caretas* (Buenos Aires), May 25, 1927 (vol. 1, 494).

debated national identity, with some questioning the mass immigration of Europeans and the understanding of Argentina as a European nation. These critics underlined Argentina's mestizo roots, harkening back to the Incas and developing ties with folklore groups and the *indigenista* movement in Peru. As was the case during the 1810s and 1820s, those more sympathetic to this position supported Juan Bautista.[54]

Blomberg also lamented that "no Lord Byron has sung the long tragedy of the Inca in chains"[55] There actually might have been a connection between Rivadavia, Juan Bautista, and the English Romantic poets. Rivadavia was in France and above all England from 1814 to 1821 and became intrigued by English poets such as Lord Byron, Keats, and Shelley. He appreciated their critical and even disruptive tone in conservative England, and the Romantics' passion for travel and history. Lord Byron had admired the Spanish American independence movements and expressed his desire of "climbing the Andes, and ascending the Oronoco."[56] Perhaps Rivadavia's experience led him to support Juan Bautista, in search of an Andean epic.[57]

Just as the plans to import an Inca monarch by Belgrano and his supporters in 1816 and the support shown for Juan Bautista a few years later prompted fierce criticism, this resurgence of interest in *Forty Years* had its detractors. In 1935, Argentine historian Juan Canter wrote, "the subject [Juan Bautista] was incapable of writing the memoirs." Canter described how "this Indian knew how to cover up his identity and profit from this fake situation." In Canter's view, Juan Bautista was part of a nineteenth-century tradition of fake autobiographies, particularly by purported former slaves. He believed that Juan Bautista was an impostor.[58] A century after the publication of *Cuarenta años*, Argentine intellectuals remained divided about Juan Bautista

---

[54] Zoila Mendoza, *Creating Our Own: Folklore, Performance, and Identity in Cuzco, Peru* (Durham, NC: Duke University Press, 2008), esp. chapters 1–2; Alejandra Mailhe, "Ricardo Rojas: viaje al interior, la cultura popular y el inconsciente," *Anclajes*, XXI, 1 (2017), 21–42.

[55] Blomberg provides a fine reading of the memoirs. He incorrectly states, however, that Juan Bautista returned to Peru and died there. Héctor Pedro Blomberg, "Las cadenas del Inca," *La Nación* (Buenos Aires), March 23, 1930, 13.

[56] Cited in Rebecca Cole Heinowitz, *Spanish America and British Romanticism, 1777–1826: Rewriting Conquest* (Edinburgh: Edinburgh University Press, 2010), 159.

[57] This is speculative. Much more is known about Rivadavia's friendship with Jeremy Bentham. Klaus Gallo, *Bernardino Rivadavia: el primer presidente argentino* (Buenos Aires: EDHASA, 2012). On romanticism in Argentina, see Jorge Myers, "La revolución de las ideas: La generación romántica de 1837 en la cultura y en la política argentinas," in *Nueva Historia Argentina. Revolución, República, Confederación (1806–1852)*, ed. Noemí Goldman (Buenos Aires: Sudamericana, 1998, t. III); Daisy Hay, *Young Romantics: The Tangled Lives of English Poetry's Greatest Generation* (New York: Farrar, Straus and Giroux, 2010).

[58] Canter, "El raro folleto," 378–390, quote from 385. On hoaxes and impostors, see Christopher L. Miller, *Impostors: Literary Hoaxes and Cultural Authenticity* (Chicago: University of Chicago Press, 2018), especially Part 1.

Illustration by Luis Macaya, in Héctor Pedro Blomberg, "Las cadenas del Inca" (The Inca's Chains), *La Nación* (Buenos Aires), March 23, 1930.

Tupac Amaru and Inca nationalism. These texts very likely inspired Francisco Loayza, who resurrected Juan Bautista in his 1941 edition.[59]

Loayza was an iconoclastic Peruvian author and diplomat who served as Peru's consul in Seville from 1933 to 1936, just before Spain's civil war. In the late 1920s and early 1930s he was a journalist in Lima. In 1930 he launched a newspaper, *La Libertad*, which was shut down by the government a year later. Lima writers actively followed Argentine intellectual currents and Loayza, in both Lima and Seville, would have had access to periodicals such as *La Nación* and *Caras y Caretas* as well as Canter's work. Once in Sevilla in 1933 as Peru's consul, Loayza discovered rich material about the Tupac Amaru Rebellion. From 1934 through March 1936, he and his daughter

---

[59]   Loayza, *Cuarenta años.*

La Recoleta Cemetery, Buenos Aires, September 1827, annotation of death of Juan Bautista Tupamaro.

María Emelia Loayza photographed thousands of documents from the great colonial repository, the Archivo de Indias. In an April 1936 letter, he claimed that he had copied "30,000 documents," many of them on the "magnificent hero and glorious martyr José Gabriel Tupac Amaru."[60] Loayza would edit approximately a dozen books of documents on topics ranging from the Conquest to the Tupac Amaru Rebellion in his series, "The Small Great Books of American History" ("small" refers to the series' 5-by-7-inch paperback format). He tells Juan Bautista's story well, refuting doubters such as Angelis and Canter and providing dozens of essential primary documents.[61] The

[60]   The Archivo General de Indias's records indicate that Francisco Loayza used the facilities from 1934 until 1936 while his daughter did so from March 1935 until June 1936. My thanks to the archivist María Teresa López Arandia for providing this material. Loayza also replicated Juan Bautista's journey from Cádiz to Ceuta, via Isla de León and Sancti Petri; Loayza, *Cuarenta años,* 52. The quotes are from his April 9, 1936 letter, Archivo Central Ministerio de Relaciones Exteriores, Servicio Consular, Consulado del Perú en Sevilla 8-14-T Entradas. I thank Ascensión Martínez Riaza for sharing this document.

[61]   Loayza deserves a biography. I found important information in his different books as well as Lidia Ruíz, "Bio-bibliografía de Francisco Loayza," *Anuario Bibliográfico Peruano, 1961–1963* (Lima: Editorial Lumen, 1966). For an obituary, see *La Prensa,* Lima, January 12, 1963.

Plaque honoring Juan Bautista Tupac Amaru, Cuzco Municipality, 1973.
Photo by Karina Pacheco Medrano.

eminent writer Alberto Tauro lauded Loayza's work in a 1942 review: "Stirring testimonies such as those found in the pages of this book compel us to honor the precursors and agents of our national independence. Its legacy takes on a renewed relevancy, commanding us to conserve and honor it."[62] Tauro pointed out that only two copies of the Buenos Aires edition were known to exist in the early 1940s. Since Loayza, editions have appeared in Chile, Argentina, and Peru. Loayza prompted a reconsideration of and deep appreciation for the life and writing of Juan Bautista.[63]

What happened to the Augustine friar and the Peruvian rebel after the publication of *Forty Years* in Buenos Aires? We know little about Durán Martel after his arrival there. One document refers to him as the chaplain of the city's general hospital in 1824.[64] Surprisingly, this hero of the 1812 Huánuco uprising and loyal companion to Juan Bautista has fallen into oblivion.

---

[62]   *Peruanidad*, (Lima) 10, September–October 1942, 863.

[63]   For an excellent analysis, particularly on Juan Bautista in Argentina, see Astesano, *Juan Bautista de América*. Other editions include Inca Juan Bautista Tupac Amaru, *Las memorias de Tupac Amaru* (Lima: Fondo de Cultura Popular, 1964); Alfredo Varela, *Memorias del hermano de Tupac Amaru Escritas en Buenos Aires* (Buenos Aires: Editorial Boedo, 1976); Hernán Neira, *Visión de los vencidos: estudio y transcripción de las memorias de Juan Bautista de Tupac Amaru* (Santiago: Editorial USACH, 2009); José Luis Ayala, *Juan Bautista Tupac Amaru* (Lima: Fondo Editorial Cultura Peruana, 2013).

[64]   *Conduct of the British Consul-General Mr. Parish to Mr. Oughgan, Surgeon, a British Subject in Buenos Ayres* (London: J. Innes, Printer, 1824), 39.

Juan Bautista wrote to Simón Bolívar in May 1825 requesting help to return to his homeland, Peru. Addressing Bolívar as the Liberator of Perú, he explained, "I have made it to the age of eighty-six, despite great hardships and threats to my life, to see consummated the great and always just struggle that will grant us in the full enjoyment of our rights and liberty . . . [I] harbor in my heart the sweet prospect of breathing the air of my homeland."[65] He never received a response and never returned. Juan Bautista witnessed the release of his memoirs and died on September 2, 1827. He is buried in an unmarked grave somewhere in the La Recoleta cemetery in Buenos Aires. Cuzco has honored him with several monuments, but plans to repatriate his remains have never been fulfilled.

---

[65]   CDIP 2, 3, 908–09 (reproduced in the Primary Sources section).

PART III
PRIMARY SOURCES

1. MEMOIRS

What follows is the translation of about half of Juan Bautista's memoirs, the key source for this book. He wrote them after his arrival in Buenos Aires in 1822 and they were published between 1824 and 1826. As I contend in the Historical Context section, his petitions to the Spanish courts in previous decades had served as first drafts or outlines. He and Father Durán Martel might have begun them during their long wait for permission and then a ship in Algeciras and Gibraltar or in the trip across the Atlantic. Juan Bautista Azopardo also might have collaborated.

I have prioritized the autobiographical material over his philosophical musings. Juan Bautista uses the language of the Enlightenment and the Age of Revolution, presenting his tragic life as a symbolic and painful example of the global struggle against tyranny and monarchism ("the universal conflagration with which humanity is making their thrones tremble"). He uses several light metaphors and refers to nature's struggle against the ancient regime. Juan Bautista also makes a few classical allusions, referring, for example, to Socrates and the Roman soldier Scaevola.

Juan Bautista repeatedly condemns the Spanish for their cruelty, tyranny, despotism, and more. In several passages, he asks whether the Spanish were heartless by nature, whether this trait was inherent, part of the Spaniards' constitution. He also poses the hypothesis that perhaps centuries of harsh rule in the Americas had made them cruel by tradition. His writing reflects the highly charged rhetoric of the 1820s in Spanish America, as countries from Mexico to Argentina had recently gained independence after a decade of warfare or more. He wrote his memoirs for publication in Argentina, at a point when critiques of the Spanish would have been well received. But his tone and content cannot be dismissed as mere nationalist slander aimed to please his benefactors and potential readers in Argentina. A minor participant in the Tupac Amaru Rebellion, Juan Bautista had witnessed the ghastly deaths of his extended family and had spent almost forty years in a variety of wretched jails on both sides of the Atlantic. To condemn the Spanish, he did not have to exaggerate or invent, but simply to tell his life story, which he did with style and precision.

As an 80-year-old who spent 40 years in prison for the cause of independence, I find myself transported from the abysm of servitude to the heights of freedom, inspired by new winds, encouraged to introduce myself to a new generation as a victim of despotism who, to the amazement of humanity, has survived its blows. I am eager to reveal the secret of my existence, an exquisite and ferocious example orchestrated by the tyrants for the pleasure of embittering me.[1]

Three Spanish Kings have taken pleasure in my miserable and humble existence; the reasons for my chains had been forgotten and almost all the institutions themselves had changed due to the passing of time and the succession of monarchs, and only I was kept without freedom for their entertainment. This example of the Kings' ferocity would have remained hidden among so many other cases of their suffocating power had it not been for the universal conflagration with which humanity is making their thrones tremble, weakening Spain's monarchs. I owe my freedom to these transformations; otherwise I would have never attained it. I offer my gratitude to those behind this new march of humanity and my strongest hope that they finish the work of the enlightenment; to all of them, this history of my suffering.

In this already violent context, King Charles III sent a commissioner named José Antonio de Areche, with the title of Visitador, to establish state monopolies, custom houses, sales taxes etc. throughout Peru. These rapacious measures by the Spanish, opening the doors to their greed, set off the desperation of the indigenous people. On October 4, 1780 my brother put himself at the head of 25,000 Indians. He led this holy insurrection, as nature began the regeneration of mankind, their efforts foreshadowing world happiness.

But justice does not always prevail, and although the Indians fought against their oppressors with admirable courage, they did not have the skill of killing as many as possible in the shortest time, because they had inherited from their parents the notions of justice, frugality, sweetness of character, and love for work and for their fellow creatures. Their virtue and their rights were thus quickly open to attack. They no doubt had the resolution of Scaevola and the virtue of Socrates yet they fell prey to their enemies' power and thirst for

---

[1] Juan Bautista errs repeatedly about his age, calling himself an octogenarian when in fact he was still in his seventies. This seems an understandable mistake for someone who had no access to written records about his life and times. Perhaps he added a few years to increase the drama of his story. Only the most coldhearted reader could criticize him for this.

revenge. The Spanish allowed their passions to run wild, killing hundreds of families without considering age or gender. Terror spread and the Spanish took advantage of this degrading emotion, arranging for the perfidious betrayal of my brother by one of his *compadres* in the town of Langui.

At this point the tigers sharpened their claws and let nothing get in the way of their ferocity: they took my brother Tupac Amaru, his wife Micaela Bastidas, their children Fernando and Hipólito, his brother-in-law Antonio Bastidas, and other family members to Cusco. Visitador Areche had Tupac Amaru appear covered in chains and, with the ferocity and arrogance of a despot, asked him about his accomplices. Tupac Amaru answered that he did not know them by sight. Areche lined up all of the respectable citizens of Cuzco for him to identify, to which my brother, with noble contempt, told him, "the only accomplices here are you and I; you for oppressor and I for Liberator, and we deserve death."

[Areche] imposed death sentences on my brother and his family, carried out with a horrible mix of torture. Tupac Amaru's wife, Micaela Bastidas, was guillotined, while their sixteen-year-old son, Fernando, his brother-in-law Antonio Bastidas, and other family members were hanged. My brother had to witness this spectacle, made even worse by the attendance of numerous people enslaved to the Spanish, calm and obedient spectators whose passivity gave it an air of triumph.[2]

And all of this was just the prelude of what was to come: Spanish cruelty deemed to have Tupac Amaru tied up and suspended at a medium height and then released so that his own weight would result in broken bones, bruises, and other bodily harm. They repeated this vicious invention for three days, delighted by the toll it took, asking him about his accomplices and funding. His philosophical answers and firmness in responding in the midst of the worst torture made them recognize an elevated soul, superior to their barbarism. Irritated that they could not get a confession from him that would have satisfied their greed and increased the number of victims, they ordered that executioners extract his tongue . . . then tied his arms and legs to four horses and quartered him. . . .[3]

---

[2]   Juan Bautista get some facts wrong about the rebellion, particularly the execution of his brother and Micaela Bastidas in 1781. This makes sense—he did not witness these events and tells the story more than forty years later. As Francisco Loayza argued in his 1941 edition of the memoirs, these discrepancies and minor errors actually support the argument that Juan Bautista was the author. It is natural that he got some details wrong. Francisco Loayza, *Cuarenta años de cautiverio*, 22.

[3]   The excruciating torture with the strappado, or *garrucha*, took place on late April 29 and the execution on May 18, 1781. Walker, *The Tupac Amaru Rebellion*, 156–167.

I wasn't in prison at this point and thus avoided the canine furor that the Spanish have always displayed when they have men in their clutches. But the display of my brother's limbs in the entryways to Cuzco; the annihilation of a distinguished and innocent family that had maintained the ancient Incas'—our virtuous ancestors—purity, humility, and sweetness, because of my brother's magnanimous resolution to break the chains imposed by greed and fanaticism, the weight of which facilitate the progress of immorality; the bitter horror of seeing Spanish arrogance triumphantly committing new crimes; all of this broke my heart. . . .

Only a few days after the disastrous death of my brother, the treachery of a few women resulted in my capture in the hills of Surimana. I was chained, my house profaned, my possessions sacked, all by my countrymen, friends, and dependents. Having found 100* pesos [*amount was really 134], the captors tortured me, jamming my pinkies in a musket trigger and squeezing until they were convinced that I didn't have any more money. As soldiers with bayonets escorted me to Cusco, people screamed insults at me. I was dumped into a dark and filthy dungeon, incommunicado, treated worse than my companions, thieves and assassins. I spent a year there, always hungry, eating bits of rotten food thrown out at the market. If I heard human voices, it was the insults of the criminals around me. They also called me a rebel and traitor.

The day they executed don Pedro Mendigure, my cousin Doña María Cecilia Tupac Amaru's husband, they paraded María and me around on burros, whipping us. What stood out is that these men took pleasure in my humiliation and torment, even laughing at it, like the conquistadors who hunted Indians with dogs for fun. This ferocity had been passed on, almost by contagion, to Indians themselves, who by nature are humane and sweet . . . Some gave me compassionate looks while those who had become soldiers either insulted me with scorn or looked at me with unbearable disdain. The young men who for their skin color or for their less humble ways were closer to the Spanish were insolent, insulting me. . . .

After a year of this suffering, I was sentenced to six years in a presidio. Visitador Areche wanted me dead while Commander Gabriel de Avilés defended me, ultimately freeing me. I returned home a changed man: justice seemed to be an illusion, men wild beasts, tyrants monsters. In light of this existential crisis, I decided to focus on my family and, if I met them, those who had suffered like me; I was so weak that it took us six days to walk the eighty-five miles from Cuzco to our house.[4]

For a year we struggled to have enough to eat, ill at ease, confronting all types of difficulties just to get by. Rumors, the distancing of our best friends,

---

4   Fourteen miles a day is a respectable pace in this mountainous area, but slow for rural folk such as Juan Bautista and Susana Aguirre.

almost generalized contempt, and the painful proscriptions we faced, some based on fear and some on hatred, made us think that the worst was still to come, despite King Charles III's word, who promised us safety.

I was apprehended and we were all taken to Cuzco, with the most sinister of omens: our captors insulted us in vile fashion on the journey. They took everything from our houses: horses, mules, and silver, dividing the plunder. What could we keep? They placed us, our friends and families, in already prepared jail cells. They executed my cousin Diego Cristóbal, displaying his head and body parts in Cuzco's entryways. His mother, wife, sisters, and brothers- and sisters-in-law suffered the same fate. For some notable reason that I will never be able to explain, I was not involved in this butchery, although in a show of animosity, a sacrilegious hand set fire to my house and salted my fields. The Pomacanchi priest did this. . . .

Sentenced to perpetual exile, our day of departure arrived. . . .

More than sixty unlucky and miserable souls left from Cuzco, including children from three to eight years old, all shackled. Our tears and moans, our tattered clothing, our cadaver-like appearance from the hunger and thirst that they forced on us, did not prompt any type of compassion. To the contrary, insults rained down on us: "scoundrels, traitors, you should pay for it." We were paraded around Cuzco's Plaza de Armas to display our degradation, our chains, the foreboding of our ruin, as the Spanish showed off their inhumanity and baseness to a degraded people.

One humane act by a single Indian among 6,000 people is worth noting. He had to struggle against his fear of persecution and the disdain of the crowd yet, in the end, the tyrants could not prevent this moral victory. Overcome with friendship and passion, this commendable man approached me as we were being paraded around the plaza and handed me a horse . . . which saved me from some of the misery my comrades had to endure. They suffered with their horses, as the captives' heavy chains, their lack of riding experience, and their oppressors' nonstop screams and ridicule made the trip unbearable and dangerous.[5] Every fall meant not only scrapes and sores from the chains and shackles which tormented them but also the furious abuse of the soldiers who got them back up with blows from their muskets and bayonets. My 125-year-old uncle, Don Bartolomé Tupac Amaru, was not exempted from the soldiers' abuse. In our entire trip to Lima through many towns, we always stayed in dungeons or cells, watched over by men whose profession seemed to be that of tormenting humanity. I don't remember receiving any sign of interest from the people of these different towns, even

---

[5]   Juan Bautista refers to horses but other documents mention mules.

though our entrances were noisy and should have moved the soul of anyone not degenerated by despotism.

In one place, someone sent us some liquor which our commander prohibited us from drinking. For that single act of compassion, I can confirm that in every town we thereafter suffered terribly. Our guides competed to see who could be the cruelest: they had us go two or three days without eating or drinking; they answered our urgent pleas for help with blows and insults; and their insensitivity, or better their complacency and denaturalization in mortifying us, reached the point that my poor mother, Ventura Monjarrás, begged for water for three days, with desperation, tears, and the sounds that only a dying body can produce. We could not help her despite our anguished pleas to our oppressors, but they, what horror, watched her die, as she begged, "water, water." Although they seemed to hear her in her final moments, it was too late: she died of dehydration and her loss inflicted on us an indescribable oppression. She was the victim of shocking insensitivity by those who were in charge of our well-being. I still cannot understand even today how so many men could partake in such cruel insensitivity. Could it be true that the Spanish are cruel by constitution? Our entire trip to Lima was an opportunity for them to develop this trait.

The trip took forty days. We thought that with the arrival to the capital, where we believed that the most reasoned and eminent authorities resided, our treatment would improve. How foolish we were! Only the torturers and tortures changed in Lima. Our cell was the most melancholic that could be constructed by man: we were tied to a chain that ran down the middle and our guard was told to impale us if we moved at all. The execution of this order was flexible, depending on the will of the guard. One guard's greed led him to continually test how much we could suffer, as he prevented us from making the most natural movements in order to force us to cough up bribes.

A series of horrific cruelties sought to impress on us our absolute impotence. It would take too long to chronicle them all but I cannot overlook those that were repeated daily and made a long-lasting impression on me. One was the challenge to our modesty as we had to witness or suffer the presence of our comrades doing their daily necessities; the other was coming down with malaria, whose symptoms include constant shaking. I can still recall suffering with these due to our chains and our generally terrible situation, which prompted only laughter from our guards. Many comrades died around us including my uncle Bartolomé Tupac Amaru, who was 125. We all got malaria because of the lack of exercise, the filthy food, the bad air that we breathed, and above all the worst impressions that affected us at all times.[6]

---

6   Juan Bautista twice uses the term *impresiones*, the notion that negative feelings or experiences could worsen one's health. It might have been related to the indigenous concept of *susto*, the notion that the soul leaves the body after a trauma or fright, prompting lethargy and ennui.

We spent five months in Lima's dungeons. Our departure from the Callao docks repeated the scene in Cuzco: the new circumstances, however, gave our tyrants the opportunity to implement new forms of torture. Shackled, we hobbled along towards the boat, driven by bayonets. One young man in the crowd, moved by our suffering, gave me his hand to keep me upright, preventing more bayonet blows from falling on my back.

My family and I were placed on the frigate *El Peruano*; other comrades were on the *San Pedro de Alcántara*. The Captain of the *El Peruano* Don José Córdova was particularly fierce.[7] He had all the defects of his nationality (he was a Spaniard): superstitious, amoral, inhumane, greedy. . . . We depended on him for all our necessities and the rumor that we had committed some crime inspired the spirit of revenge in him, which he displayed throughout our entire voyage.

We were all placed on the main deck, chained to one another with no more protection than an old poncho and a sheepskin. Our food was so meager that we were always hungry and we scrambled for the bones that the crew threw towards us when they cooked, even though we understood that they did it out of contempt, to treat us like dogs. We were so desperate that we considered them a treat. We suffered numerous illnesses due to the unhealthy air and the irritating impressions that we experienced, and our complete neglect only made things worse. The doctor, the chaplain, and the commander never gave us the aid corresponding to their duties. Half of my comrades died of scurvy before we reached Rio de Janeiro, two of them dying right next to me, actually chained on top of me, remaining there until the following morning. All of them were victims of this noteworthy and inhumane neglect. My wife, whose affection and circumstances inspired me, also died; this privation of my last bit of solace so ravished my spirit that with all sincerity I wanted to die. Spouses who are close will be able to understand my situation in those moments. What cruelty by our oppressors.

A nephew of mine who was cramped and in pain with colic received only laughter and cold indifference from our guides, and he died in the middle of a storm due to this ailment. Witnessing him suffer and receive no help was a true torture for us. Some of my comrades, motivated by the violence of our situation and our boredom, sent a petition to our commander, which should have moved even the most insensitive heart. With pitiful submission, it requested some improvement in our conditions. The answer was, "the supplicant will abstain from any more petitions, if not, he and all his comrades will be tied to the cannons." This decree embittered us greatly; it smothered any

---

7   José de Córdova y Ramos de Garay (1732–1815) had a long career in the Spanish Navy, both in the Indies fleet as well as in frequent wars with England; *Diccionario Biográfico electrónico*, s.v. "José de Córdova y Ramos de Garay," accessed December 9, 2019, http://dbe.rah.es/biografias/15033/jose-de-cordova-y-ramos-de-garay.

hopes we had as we realized that in Spain our suffering would not end. There, they would continue to prohibit our requests, understand the inhumanity of the commander and other authorities as laudable zeal, and ignore anyone with a heart who complained about our situation.

We made it to Rio de Janeiro where the ship docked for repairs. Half of my comrades were dead. The rest were in very bad shape and some women were sent to a hospital. They returned two days later, embittered by the abandonment and bad treatment by the Portuguese, either because of the commander's recommendation or the particular nature of the Portuguese. One of the women died as soon as she returned on deck.

Despite being ill, the rest of us weren't treated any better than before. In fact, they took even more terrorizing precautions. During the day we were tied to the mast and at night tied up on deck. Nothing, not even rain and the rigors of the sun or our inadequate clothing, relieved us from this . . . One priest who came with us from Lima endeavored so that we could wash our ragged clothes, which were unbearably filthy. We had worn them since our capture and the sweating and humidity etc. made them wretched. In all this time, we had not had a change of clothes or bedding.

We were in Rio for four months and then set out for Spain, which was at war with England. This meant that an English ship could possibly seize ours and free us. Any time the commander saw a ship or conceived of any type of danger, even if only in his fantasies, we were all tied to the main mast. The crew reacted furiously to these announcements: they showed us their bayonets, making it clear they were ready and willing to plunge them through us; that was their language. It pleased them to see our almost naked bodies, always hungry and thirsty, suffer with the water, the heat, and the cold. When I tried to alleviate my suffering, I paid for it dearly.

A comrade offered me some crackers, telling me to hurry before the guards came. We were about to be returned to the walkway so although I was weak and shackled, I scuttled over and managed to put a few in my hat. Meanwhile, the guard had maneuvered the hatch in such a way that when I took a seat, I fell to the hull of the ship, landing on some ropes and breaking two ribs. My pain, the chains, and my general weakness meant that I was in agony and only my comrades offered any type of help. The crew impeded them, however, from fulfilling the compassion my groans prompted. One crew member, however, was sensitive to my plight and gave me a hand up. The others laughed about my entanglement in the ropes and in general my conditions didn't change. The surgeon and commander didn't offer to help and the only medicine I received was a bit of tar from the caulker to use as a balm. I had to rely on nature. I got better but not fully recovered as even today I'm still sore in that area and the pain flares up easily.

Before finishing about the Rio to Cádiz leg of the journey, I want to tell one story that captures the tyranny of those in charge. Spaniards' adhesion to prayer is well known, it's the essence of their religiosity as morality is a much lower priority. Even so, when they saw us pray the rosary to gain some type of solace, they prohibited us from doing so. I should point out that these Spaniards were coarse, ignorant, and superstitious, like most of them who came to the Americas. . . .

After more than ten months of navigation since our departure from Lima, we reached Cádiz with the hope that our suffering would end, persuaded that whatever the King thought about our supposed crimes, he would realize that we had already paid for them with all that we had suffered (as though Kings born and raised in luxury and comfort had any notion of common people' suffering, in order to compare and analyze). Furthermore, since we hadn't had any type of trial that would have reviewed our crimes, there was no evidence that could be reviewed, that humanity might consider.

We disembarked on March 1, 1785, and I was taken shackled with twenty-five pounds of chains to San Sebastián Castle. I was in such bad shape that having gone out for nightly prayers I reached the castle at midnight, as two grenadiers had to hold me by the arms so that I could walk. They had made special cells for us. These rooms, if they could be called that, contained all of life's destructive principles: stone walls, with small holes for two iron beams in the form of a cross; humid floors also made of stone, and double doors. We were separated, with most of my comrades placed in the Santa Catalina Castle. Mine had a small pallet for my bed, composed as I've said of a sheepskin and some rags, all filthy and stinky. These were all my possessions with which I had to confront a life surrounded by cruel enemies. Guards were placed at the door, the small hole that served as a window, and on the roof. They took these precautions for my arrival from such a great distance. I was overwhelmed by exhaustion but was given no food.

You can imagine my situation having been transported to such a remote place, surrounded by guards, with no knowledge of the town, separated from the consolation of my comrades in misery; alone, hungry, and realizing in this bleak context that my future was dreadful.

I was treated better when the Swiss Guard or other foreigners were in charge. They allowed us to get some sun, showed some compassion, and never took anything from us, in contrast to the Spanish sentinels.

I don't remember any human touch by any Spaniard in charge of guarding me in my three years and three months in San Sebastián.

[In 1788,] After four or five days when I was sure they going to execute me, they put me on a ship to the Isla de León, with no cover from the sun and unbearable hunger and thirst. I went down a long street to a river where they put me on another boat and after many turns we reached Sancti Petri. You can imagine my concern with these endless trips, in which they treated me inhumanely, as badly as they could. I thought that if for my brother they used various forms of torture—pulling out his tongue, quartering him alive, etc.— then for me they would come up with even more barbarous inventions or even crueler tricks.

From Sancti Petri I was taken to Ceuta, traveling on top of the salt that the ship carried as cargo. I arrived after four days at sea, June 1, 1788. News about my arrival brought everyone out to see me. Although I was mixed together with the assassins and thieves brought on the same ship, my physiognomy was very different than that of the Europeans and everyone stared, some treating me as an object of curiosity, some to point out in my profile the infallible signs of a soul perverse by nature, others to deny me the considerations any man deserved. They claimed that I was undeserving because I was an *Americano* and thus excluded from any compassion. All looked at me like a criminal, because they saw me being punished. If they all believed that their King was sent by God to govern, how could they doubt that I was guilty?[8]

Guards, virtual executioners, came to meet their victims. The ferocity in their faces showed that their job was to torment prisoners. One of them, who looked hungrier than the prisoners, ordered us to follow him. The captain of our ship, however, said that I was different and took me to meet Ceuta's governor, Don Miguel Porcel y Manrique de Arana, Conde de las Lomas, telling him that I was not the same as the other common prisoners and that I should be separated from them. The governor instructed his assistant to place me in a private house.

A silversmith who happened to be there offered to take me. The way he treated me made me realize that he did so in order to get in the good graces of the governor rather than because of any type of compassion. I never had a set

---

[8]   I have kept the term *Americanos*, referring to all people born in the Americas, rather than translating it to Americans. The latter might lead readers to think of the United States, an unfortunate but prevalent interpretation. Juan Bautista was proud of his friendship with figures such as the Maltese Argentine Juan Bautista Azopardo or the Bolivian Mariano Subieta and understood that Americano solidarity helped get his beloved Marcos Durán Martel and him out of Ceuta and to freedom in Argentina. In fact, he closes by underlining how much Americanos could learn from Durán Martel's example of selfless generosity.

place to sleep or for myself and my primary necessities were done according to my new masters' whims. If they remembered, I ate; if not, I went hungry. One day because I spit on one part of the floor rather than another, it prompted such a row with the silversmith's wife that I asked the Governor's assistant if I could live on my own. He accepted with the condition that I present myself twice a week at headquarters.

In this new situation I realized for different reasons how marginal or even useless the government's measures had made me. I didn't know Spanish and that nation's customs.[9] I couldn't be completely self-reliant and had to deal with others. Despite all my precautions, I was surrounded by tricks, bad faith, and greed, as vile men sought to rob my meager money, always with a facade of friendship, the easiest way to lure a broken and lonely heart like mine.

I understood the world I was in, the atmosphere in which I breathed, when my efforts to gain an education, which in light of my circumstances and dedication would have made me more competent, were met with scorn and ridicule . . . Desperate to fulfill this goal, I took the correct decision, that of living alone, as society offered me nothing but oppressors and disappointments. I rented a small field to cultivate on my own, an assiduous occupation that wouldn't force me to deal with Europeans who treated me so inhumanely. This type of death or isolation explains my survival and my experience ultimately justified the decision. Nonetheless, my decision to isolate myself meant that my memories of the calamities I had undergone and had put me in Ceuta tormented me even more.

Over my thirty-two years in Ceuta I had many bitter experiences but two stand out. One day needing to get out I went to watch military exercises, even though I was oddly horrified by these professional assassins, especially after I learned that in Europe men sold themselves to the highest bidder to fight for whatever cause, that it wasn't defending their flag that attracted them but rather the amount of money offered. One day these men would defend one cause and the next day the opposite one, to only later go back to the first one.

You can imagine my surprise and terror when I was watching the military exercises, in the middle of the crowd, and a commander pulled me apart from the others and started bashing me with his staff, leaving me stunned and then unconscious. All of those around me were shocked and I left without knowing the cause of his outburst, with nowhere to lodge a complaint. I could only explain it by my all-so Americano features, which had infuriated this officer, a common reaction among Spaniards when confronted with an Indian. I learned a few days later that he had suddenly died, but no doubt not regretting what he had done to me.

---

[9]   Francisco Loayza contends that Juan Bautista spoke Spanish well but endeavored to become more literate. In this passage, Juan Bautista exaggerates his ignorance of Spanish. Loayza, *Cuarenta años de cautiverio*, 52–54.

But what was much more unbearable was when I ran into an Indian on the street and he asked me if I were from Cuzco. I said that I was Tupac Amaru and he furiously asked how I was still alive, that I should have died long ago. I expected this fellow Indian to answer my friendly response with some sensitivity but it hurt me to understand that he was a denaturalized enemy of mine, his vile arrogance leaving me with a bitter taste for days.

But on June 1, 1813 Don Marcos Durán Martel introduced himself to me, a man who atoned for all of those who had hurt me so. He proved himself a guiding hand destined to save me, to allow me to enjoy in my final years the wonders of friendship.

He introduced himself as an Americano persecuted by tyranny, just like me. I offered him my house, the hospitality of a friend, I poured my heart out to him. We did everything together, like brothers, although he did more: seeing that as an octogenarian, I had difficulty working my plot of land, he took over and ended up doing all the work. He made sure that I was at peace and comfortable. It is laudable how much care and effort he put into this, for which he received nothing except his heart's satisfaction.

I had lost any hope of regaining freedom but Durán Martel provided such a rosy picture of the birth, spirit, and progress of revolution in the Americas that the prospect of returning to Peru prompted the most extraordinary and healthy reawakening of my soul, particularly for someone my age. My body was no longer tired and I had new and sweet feelings that I hadn't felt for forty years; the world and my situation were totally new.

My hope of returning to the Americas was reborn and became my greatest desire. Despite so many years living with Europeans, I had not bonded with anything or anyone. In this regard, I was the same after half a life in Europe and Ceuta as the day I arrived. If anything, my heart was bitter over the mistreatment I had suffered and the aversion these beasts could inspire. . . .

Even though my remarkable friend's stories about the state of the Americas were inspiring and they made me cry tears of affection (they reminded me of the disastrous fate of my brother and others who sacrificed their lives, yet also showed me that there was new life in the countries where I was born), they remained mere beautiful images as I couldn't stop contrasting the state of Cuzco and the other countries when I left them with the image that Durán Martel was painting. Certainly, without the shaking up of Europe with the French Revolution, the sparkle of light wherever the fuel of human reason existed, and Spain's mistreatment of its American possessions, none of these changes would have occurred for centuries.

But the arrival of many prisoners who fought for this cause, the particularly bad treatment given to Americanos, and the sharp echoes of news from across Europe that reached the presidio every day convinced me that changes were afoot.

By 1820, my comrade Durán Martel and I became more and more hopeful about the situation in the Americas. . . . He took care of me and boosted my morale in ways I was no longer able to do for myself. I admired the conjunction of so many things going in my favor, above all his noble generosity that outdid the efforts of the best son or daughter. I did suffer when my faithful companion was thrown in jail for a few days. It was done with such a fuss that I feared the worst; however, Ceuta's Bishop intervened and saved him.

In 1820 the Spanish Parliament decreed that all American political prisoners should be freed, granting them 10 reales a day until a government ship could take them home, at no cost. Taking advantage of this effervescence, all the Americanos claimed their freedom. My comrade, however, refused to take his unless I was also cleared to go. I requested my freedom but was turned down by the comptroller Antonio García, with the pretext that I had been sentenced by the Council of the Indies, not Parliament. García did not take into account that Parliament had precedent over the Council of the Indies. His ruling was sheer animosity towards Americanos. My comrade tried to circumvent this, having me request sick leave to Algeciras where, if I wasn't granted my freedom, I could take political asylum in neighboring Gibraltar, a good place to find a ship home.

As I was walking down the dock in Ceuta about to board a ship for Algeciras, having been granted permission and leaving Don Francisco Isnardi to collect my pension, I had the most painful accident: I fell down eleven steps, breaking my arm and bruising my entire body.

I decided to delay my return to the Americas at this point; at my age I thought recovery from the fall would be very slow if not impossible. Also, I couldn't ask that my comrade spend more time with me and miss his departure; my heart couldn't take that Durán Martel make this sacrifice for me. I insisted that he leave me, that a subsequent change of heart by the government could mean he was forced to remain in Ceuta. My frankness only allowed me to see his magnanimity, his humanity, his generosity that in Europe would be considered chimerical. My wounds suddenly improved with his answer, as he insisted that he would not abandon me. In fact, he seemed offended and told me, "how could you imagine that I would deprive you of my care and assistance in the moments when you most needed me. I would never return to the Americas if it meant leaving you behind with your enemies and denying myself the pleasure of caring for you." He said it with such fervor that the surgeon told me that the broken bones had set so well that his services weren't needed. The power of friendship can do so much!

However, some new illnesses worsened my misery and I had to be hospitalized. How I suffered with the Spaniards' non-stop war against me. I would have died were it not for my comrade's dedication. He himself brought me my food which he prepared with his own hands, and only through his efforts did we have it because the hospital provided such miserable slop that it was better to turn it down. I was there twenty days. My partner never once let me lose hope of freedom and a return to the Americas.

Once he saw me with a bit of strength we set out to depart from Algeciras, this time with more success. I was introduced to the Puerto Rican General Don Demetrio O'Daly and this encounter with Spanish authorities was much better than previously had been the case. Furthermore, he let me move around freely which, combined with the generous hospitality of Don José Gonzalo and the openness with which the Vicar allowed Durán Martel to say Mass, our situation improved greatly. Also, my arm was better within four months.

In light of my faint health, my comrade had always hidden from me the obstacles to my freedom until they were behind us. But realizing that he needed my cooperation, Durán Martel explained to me that we still couldn't count on my freedom, and that we would have to pass from Algeciras to Gibraltar furtively. We counted on the promised support of one man. For eighteen months we survived on this hope and at the end we figured out that this man who took on the airs of a benefactor was only trying to make money from us. When he realized that we would not be able to satisfy his greed he told us he could no longer help us.

We realized that we would not be able to make our escape without spending more than we had. And our funds were declining with our long stay in Algeciras and because our representative in Ceuta, Francisco Isnardi, who gained our trust in light of his long fight for independence in Caracas, had stronger ties to his nation than he did to us and to moral codes. Isnardi denied having received any money for me. Convinced to the contrary by the treasurer's report that confirmed that Isnardi had collected my pension, we asked an authority to intervene but got nowhere. Authorities' habit of denying Americanos their rights outweighed the obvious contradiction between this official's behavior and the principles that he proclaimed.

We had only one alternative, the toughest one which we had bad premonitions about: make a formal complaint to the authorities. My comrade Durán Martel encouraged me as did my memories of the support promised by the Spanish Liberal Don Agustín Argüelles, when we had been prisoners in Ceuta together. So, I sent our petition to the Governor of Ceuta as well as to Argüelles himself. Argüelles quickly answered by sending me a certificate of my freedom and an explanatory letter.[10]

---

[10] Agustín Argüelles (1776–1844) was a leading Spanish Liberal. An important figure in the Cádiz Parliament, he was imprisoned in Ceuta in 1814 with the return of King Ferdinand VII.

With Argüelles' letter, we set out for Cádiz without a problem. There, the Port Judge ordered that I receive the 10 reales a day that the Cortes had granted Americanos in my situation, including the five months that I was owed. He instructed us to hold on to our savings in Algeciras for the trip back to the Americas, and, because no Spanish ship could go, he told the Spanish consul to search for an English one.[11]

We abided by these promises until we realized that they would never come true, and that the Court's decree granting me the money was pure rhetoric and would never be implemented, that Spaniards' old habits and concerns had returned. So, we thus faced a grave difficulty, that of paying the boat fare. The price, no matter how low, would be more than what we had saved. We had to do what we could and we asked a gentleman who told us of a ship soon to depart for Buenos Aires. He spoke to the Captain to arrange a feasible price. We agreed on it, with no comfort on board, even though I foolishly thought that perhaps my age, my long years of labor, and my situation might prompt some compassion.

We embarked on July 3, 1822. Departure was always difficult for me as it affected my mood and I was struck by a habitual malady that my misfortunes had produced: I lost my faculties and had a breakdown, perhaps because I had only perceived evil for so long. The shipmates would have returned me to shore if Durán Martel had not insisted that I would soon be better, that it was a brief setback that would pass quickly.[12]

On August 3, we set sail for South America, leaving Spain forever. As cruel as it was greedy, Spain had soaked itself with lakes of American blood, just to fill Europe with torrents of silver and gold, remaining ignorant, poor and corrupt. Spain, humanist yet superstitious, invoking religion and the Gospel to slaughter Americanos, seeking to be philosophical, with equality and the Rights of Man at the tip of their tongue, yet sending armies of tigers, from Caracas to Peru. Spain, with its unjust possession of Peru, replaced the knowledge and happiness of the ancient Incas with ignorance, despotism, and servitude, depriving humanity of the Incas' advances in the social and natural sciences. I must confess, I abandoned Spain with a sweet premonition that their misfortune due to their vices would scare off other Europeans who sought to dominate the Americas, an enterprise that is innately unjust, exploitative and other defects associated with the Spanish. If other European nations tried, they would have the same fate.

My situation on my return to South America was in some ways entirely the opposite of that of when I was sent to Spain, although in some ways it was

---

11   The Spanish–British conflict over Gibraltar impeded Spanish ships in this part of the Mediterranean in these years.

12   Juan Bautista seems to describe a nervous breakdown.

the same. I was 84 years old and for half of those years my heart had been repeatedly broken, keeping my wounds fresh and thus allowing me to understand perfectly the contrast between the care and sweetness of my companion and the tyranny and roughness of those who shipped me to Spain. And if these bad memories were fading, Captain Hague of the *Retrieve* revived them. He made me think that he was a slave trader. Our miserable condition did not stop him from collecting 200 pesos for our fare, providing us just five pounds of tobacco for our subsistence.

After ten days at sea I became so ill that I was in agony. It was due to seasickness and the terrible rations of crackers with badly cooked meat, inedible even if chewed thoroughly which I couldn't do. Also, because I was on deck with no protection from the elements, which at my age I couldn't take, I declined with extraordinary speed.

I would have died except for my comrade's care and dedication to my recovery. Durán Martel convinced the Captain to give us an egg, food that I could swallow. It restored me and without it I would have died. Neither this exemplary act of Durán Martel nor the spectacle of an eighty-year-old feeble man on the deck at risk of dying from a thousand different things made the Captain change his behavior: he kept us on the deck, never offering any type of cover even during thunderous rainstorms or when the unbearable cold hit. He offered more comfort to a dog which was on board, making it a kind of cave.

All of this motivated Durán Martel to nurture me, an old man from whom he could expect nothing in return. He preferred my comfort over his own and would run to protect me from the water or the cold, getting soaking wet himself or putting dry clothes on me. This unique man aided me in all of life's functions and I would have died going even one day without his help. When the Captain saw him work so hard for me, he asked a few people walking by who I was to deserve so much care from my comrade. The Captain could not be convinced that Durán Martel did not do it out of some ulterior motive, as Europeans are only moved by money or power.

After seventy days of navigation and only thanks to Durán Martel's generous, humanitarian efforts, I made it to Buenos Aires.

Here, my already independent brothers stretched out their arms to embrace me. My comrade, Don Mariano Subieta, also imprisoned in Europe for fighting for independence, and I were hosted with affection, friendship, and zeal by Don Juan Bautista Azopardo, who had been with us in Ceuta for the same reason.[13] The Buenos Aires Government honored us by providing Durán Martel and me with room and board and a pension. This decree was in

---

[13]   Azopardo was a Maltese Argentine navy commander who fought for Argentina during the War of Independence.

response to my request that they make my suffering their own. I expressed that arriving here was the only crown of glory that could compensate them and satisfy my heart.

The Spanish government and its rulers should be ashamed for having let me leave without righting the offense against humanity committed in my person, a national disgrace. If a forty-year jail sentence characterizes a barbarous and brutal government, the indifference regarding this conduct in a country that claims to be enlightened shows that enlightenment still hasn't taken root, that Spain's old concerns and habits are stronger than the new currents from the beginning of the century.

I paid a high price for Spain's backwardness, but it meant that my arrival to the Americas was a true triumph, achieved by my comrade Don Marcos Durán Martel. All the glory and much more goes to him, for his constant humanitarian acts, of which few men would be capable, all for a man who was on the verge of death. He brought me back to life and placed me in the midst of liberal institutions whose creation honors their founders, above all because their development irrevocably prepares our country towards unprecedented eminence; Europe will look with admiration and envy to those who it previously enslaved.

While everyone can learn from Durán Martel's behavior with me, this is particularly true of Americanos. His patriotism in Huánuco prompted the Spanish to persecute him, to send him from his birthplace to Spain and to Ceuta, where in my misery and weakness he found a vast field for his noble sentiments and magnanimous heart, allowing me to publish this history, that although tragic, will be useful to the world. I hope it makes men think about the ways to avoid tyranny that has proven so odious to me.

Francisco Loayza, ed. *Cuarenta años de cautiverio (Memorias del Inka Juan Bautista Túpac Amaru)*. Lima: Editorial Domingo Miranda, 1941.

2. COMMANDER CÓRDOBA REPORT, 1784

RIO DE JANEIRO

While in port in Rio de Janeiro, José de Córdova, the commander of *El Peruano*, reported to José de Gálvez, the Minister of the Indies and the most important figure for Spanish policy in its American holdings. Córdova included a list of the prisoners who had died of "natural illnesses," including Susana Aguirre.

Most Excellent Sir—My Lord:

For your information, I include a list of the Indians who died of natural illnesses on board this ship, en route to Spain under my command, along with

other state prisoners, on the orders of the Viceroy of Peru, as you are aware.
May God watch over Your Excellency for many years.
El Peruano. Anchored in Rio de Janeiro, August 10, 1784. . . .
José de Córdova
To: His Excellency Don Joseph de Gálvez

Information on the Indians being taken to Spain as state prisoners who have
died on the ship *El Peruano* en route from Lima to Rio de Janeiro

> Mariano Condorcanqui, died June 27
> Miguel Gutierrez, died July 21
> Isidro Pérez, died June 26
> Joseph Mamani, died July 30
> Pascual Huamán, died June 8
> Mateo Condori, died May 11
> Josef Sánchez, died June 19
> Cayetano Castro, died July 21

Their Wives

> Antonio de Castro, died May 20
> Andrea Juscamayta, died August 3
> Nicolasa Torres, died June 1
> Susana Aguirre, died April 20

Their Children, Minors:

> Gregorio Tito, died May 27
> Juliana Tito, died August 5
> María Tito, died July 10
> Feliciana Tito, died June 1.

El Peruano, Rio de Janeiro, August 10, 1784

Source: *Colección Documental de la Independencia del Perú*, Vol. 2, *La rebelión de Túpac Amaru*, 2, 3, 427–428

3. CÁDIZ PETITION, 1814

CÁDIZ, 1814

The following document confirms that Juan Bautista petitioned the Cádiz
Parliament for his freedom. King Ferdinand VII returned to power and disbanded the Parliament before its members took action regarding his plea.

Sessions, February 4, 1814

We have received a petition from Don Juan Bautista Tupac-Amaro in which he requests his freedom of which he has been deprived since 1782, having been confined to Ceuta since 1788, for no other crime, he claims, than that of being a relative of one of those involved in the commotion that took place in Cusco in the years 1780 and 1781.

Cortes. Actas de las Sesiones de la Legislatura Ordinaria de 1813–1814 (Dieron principio el 1 de Octubre de 1813 y terminaron el 19 de febrero de 1814). Tomo Único

Madrid: Imprenta y Fundición de la Viuda e Hijos de D. J. Antonio García, 1876, p. 433.

4. PETITION TO THE KING, 1814

In 1814, King Ferdinand VII was restored to power in Spain, the Napoleonic invasion defeated. He sought to reimpose Absolutism, abolishing the Liberal constitution passed by the Cádiz Parliament. As seen in the previous document, Juan Bautista had petitioned Cádiz in February 1814 but now had to reframe his request. He stressed his innocence in the Tupac Amaru Rebellion, blaming bad authorities for the uprising. He argued that King Charles III had not followed procedure in his case and that, after thirty-five years, he had suffered enough. He was correct in stating that his twenty-five-plus years in Ceuta were unique—most prisoners were there for well less than ten years.

The King did not act, and Juan Bautista and thousands of other prisoners would have to wait until the return of the Liberals in 1820.

SUMMARY ANNOTATION: Sir Juan Bautista Tupac Amaro, deprived of his freedom and property since 1782 and confined in Ceuta since 1788, requests from Your Majesty the reinstatement of the major part of his rights oppressed arbitrarily.

Sir

By a 1788 order of the Council of the Indies, I was imprisoned in this place without having committed a crime, without a sentence or a trial, for as long as the will of the then reigning Monarch deemed. In regards to this decision, taken without prior knowledge of the case, the Council of the Indies proceeded arbitrarily: just as I was deprived of a trial and a defense I was also sent to this presidio without a prior or subsequent explanation of the true motive of the punishment. I thus decided to break my long silence, communicating with the Cádiz Courts through a petition dated January 9 of this year, accompanied by the Court order, in which, without even indicating the cause for this sentence, they assigned me 6 reales a day for my sustenance. The Cádiz Courts were dismissed before they could review my petition, which forces me to bother His Majesty. I present the facts that I expressed to Cádiz, regarding the abuse of power that ripped me from my country in 1782 and that keeps me deprived of all my rights.

A solemn capitulation calmed the disturbances that the authorities of Cuzco caused there in 1780 and 1781.[1] I had nothing to do with these disturbances, but a brother of mine did, and despite being part of the capitulation, he died treacherously due to the judges in charge of administering justice there. His wife and sixteen-year-old son also died; although they committed crimes, they were protected by the amnesty. All of the others who capitulated remained immune and did not suffer. I myself was arrested when my brother died due to my last name, but was freed as I was clearly not guilty, until those same authorities, following an order from the Council of Indies, decreed that all those with my last name, as well as their families and relatives, be sent to Spain.

I was arrested and taken to Lima with my wife. My mother, father-in-law, and other relatives died on the trip. After nine months in prison and much suffering, on April 1, 1784 we were placed on a ship destined for Cádiz, without any of the procedures called for by the Laws of the Indies, and we were so mistreated in the eleven-month trip that when we reached Cádiz our numbers had greatly diminished as many had died. My wife was one of the victims, leaving me without offspring to help me work. Survivors were enclosed in the San Sebastián Castle. I remained there from February 1785 until June 1, 1788, when I was transferred here, without having been heard or interrogated and in complete isolation from others.

Since then, I have lost all contact with my relatives, lacking any communication with or support from my native land [tierra], the town of Surimana in the Canas y Canchi province, in Peru. I have lived bitterly in this presidio, particularly after the absence and captivity of Your Majesty. The 6 reales a day became even more woefully inadequate, even with the 2 real increase promised in another order, a copy of which I sent to the Cádiz Parliament. I therefore had to work doubly hard, even in my 70s, losing hope that I would ever receive the more than 10,000 reales that I was owed as well as that which I did not receive during Your Majesty's captivity.

It is above all to heaven and the virtues of your royal person that we owe the elders' restoration to the throne: and just as this will be the end of all the

---

[1]   This is a fascinating explanation of the Tupac Amaru Rebellion, putting the blame squarely on regional authorities.

misfortune that these kingdoms and those overseas have suffered, it will also be the end of my unjust exile, unique in all of your domains for its duration and its arbitrariness. The very order that imposed it should have ceased upon the death of your august grandfather [King Charles III] in that his royal determination caused my residence in this presidio. But, due to my lack of knowledge I could not petition back then, and as the paternal heart of Your Majesty is curing the wounds of the past, I hope for my complete freedom, which I plead and beg for devotedly.

In Ceuta.

June 17, 1814

Sir

At the royal feet of Your Majesty,

Juan Tupac Amaru

Archivo de Indias, Indiferente Leg. 1351

5. DURÁN MARTEL LETTER, 1814

FR. MARCOS DURÁN MARTEL

For his participation in the Huánuco rebellion of 1812, the Lima High Court (or Audiencia) sentenced Friar Marcos Durán Martel to ten years in the Ceuta presidio and banned him from holding mass. He arrived at Ceuta in 1813. In this plea to King Ferdinand VII, who had recently returned to the throne after the expulsion of the Napoleonic invasion, Durán Martel casts the Huánuco uprising as a defense of the King against nefarious usurpers. He used the language of the Cádiz Parliament. In reality, Huánuco was a radical Indian-based uprising against Spaniards. King Ferdinand had little sympathy for the Liberal Juntas and, not surprisingly, did not amend the friar's sentence.

Ceuta

July 8, 1814

Sir, Friar Marcos Martel, priest, member of the Saint Augustine Order in Huánuco, his birthplace, in the Viceroyalty of Lima, lays himself at the feet of His Majesty, to declare: I find myself in the Ceuta presidio having been sentenced by the Lima High Court to ten years in a Spanish hospital, with no return to Peru. This was one of the clauses in the High Court's sentence against several individuals who sought a government that would better defend His Majesty's rights during his absence and captivity, individuals who also counted on solid evidence not to trust the authorities who appeared in those

Kingdoms [Spanish America]. They also mistrusted the Viceroys, Ministers, and Governors who depended on these authorities. These individuals understood the danger they ran of being imprisoned by the intruder [Napoleon], not so much due to the strength of the tyrant but rather the intrigues of the Spanish emissaries and agents. Thus, concerned about the invaders' preponderance of arms as well as their domination of the entire Iberian Peninsula and desire to replicate this in the Americas, these individuals sought precautious measures that would provide security. The most opportune was that of Juntas or Assemblies in your royal name, such as those elected in Spain, but due to an inconsistency in principles, what was here proclaimed as an act of patriotism, was in Spain seen as an act of rebellion. . . .

It is therefore even more unjust to have sentenced this priest to this presidio's hospital, where he has been since June of last year, getting by on a prisoner's miserable rations, unable to even get permission to hold Mass and excluded from the income of a chaplain. . . .

Your Majesty has been restored to remedy these and other wrongdoings caused by his absence and captivity, thus the exponent pleads with great respect that His Majesty relieve him from his sentence . . . and allow him to resume his functions as a Priest.

Fray Marcos Duran Martel

Dunbar Temple, Ella, ed. *Conspiraciones y rebeliones en el siglo XIX. La Revolución de Huánuco, Panataguas y Huamalíes.* Colección Documental de la Independencia del Perú 1 (III). Lima: Comisión Nacional del Sesquicentenario de la Independencia del Perú, 1971, (Feb. 18, 1812), tomo 2, 65.

6. PETITION TO THE KING, 1821

This document from Seville's rich Archivo de Indias summarizes the paper trail for Juan Bautista's request for freedom. It includes Juan Bautista's own brief, which stresses that he was imprisoned on the whim of King Charles III thirty-five years earlier and that the King's decision, as well as the more recent one to exclude him from the amnesty laws, were unfair and illegal. Different authorities pass his plea up toward the Court in Madrid, using language that demonstrates Spain's Liberal turn in the early 1820s.

Juan Tupac Amaru
File on Juan Bautista Tupac Amaru's request to return, confined for thirty years in Ceuta. 1821

Sir Governor and General Commander:

Don Juan Tupac Amaru from Cusco, Peru and confined in this presidio for more than thirty years without any type of a sentence other than the will of King Charles III due to having the last name Tupac Amaru, a family that provoked the King's indignation, respectfully expounds: his long and unjust deportation was the result of political opinions and events and thus he is eligible for inclusion in the amnesty law for all overseas dissidents.

He requests that Your Honor declare him free in light of the forementioned amnesty law and order that he be given a passport in order to arrange transportation to the Americas in the most convenient port. He awaits the decision of His Honor. Ceuta November 30, 1820

Juan Tupac Amaru

It is confirmed that he was sent to Spain by a January 20, 1788 Royal Order, assigned a pension of 6 reales daily for food.

On December 4, 1820, the Ceuta auditor, Francisco Cano, expressed to this jurisdiction in his own handwriting that although the amnesty only corresponded to those who had recently incurred in excesses and not those as in this case who have for many years been enduring long sentences, "in light of the extended time that he has subsisted in Ceuta, I judge him worthy of presenting his case to Your Majesty to see if Your Excellecy will deign to grant him his freedom."

The Ceuta Governor, Fernando Butrón, expresses the following:

> Although the long and almost unprecedented confinement that Don Juan Tupac Amaru has endured in this presidio was in my judgement more than sufficient reason to end his suffering in light of the current liberal system that prohibits such procedures, I, however, wanted to hear the report of my auditor, which appears in these files. Agreeing with him, I pass the file along to the hands of Your Excellency for his review, so that in light of its nature, of the circumstances of both Spains, and the irreprehensible conduct of this seventy-year old, who has been confined in this presidio for more than thirty years, for three consecutive Kings, that you submit it for His Majesty's consideration, for him to resolve in the way that he sees fit.

The Secretary of State in the War division Cayetano Valdés forwards it on December 16, 1820 to the Overseas division to present it to His Majesty.

The King agrees and gives a Royal Order dated January 2, 1821 to Valdés so that he can communicate it to the Chief of Ceuta and alert Juan Tupac Amaru to select a port in which to embark. The same day the Viceroy of Peru was informed of the resolution.

On January 31, 1821, Valdés reports that Tupac Amaru has selected Cádiz for his port of departure.

Archivo General de Indias, Lima, Legajo 1023

7. *DIARIO CONSTITUCIONAL*, BARCELONA, 1821

THE PRESS

Liberals ruled Spain from 1820 to 1823. In 1820 and 1821, Liberal newspapers in Barcelona, Madrid, and Cádiz published sympathetic stories on Juan Bautista. They reproduced almost intact the first text, found in the *Tertulia Patriótica* (the Patriotic Conversation) from the Isla de León, what is now known as San Fernando Island in Cádiz. While a copy of the *Tertulia* could not be located, the stories in *Miscelánea de Comercio, Política y Literatura* (Madrid, #333, January 26, 1821), and the *Diario Constitucional* (Barcelona, #37, February 6, 1821) recount his odyssey in great detail. The *Cetro Constitucional, Seminario Político*, #1, (Madrid 1820) provides a less detailed account.

These articles must have derived from an interview with Juan Bautista or a text that he, perhaps with Durán Martel, provided. Juan Bautista had been presenting his case in the Spanish courts for almost a decade. These petitions and texts constitute first drafts of his memoirs. They contain the same storyline, even getting similar facts wrong about the Tupac Amaru Rebellion. Liberal Spain sought to highlight the plight of martyrs and victims of the Old Regime, and Juan Bautista was a compelling example.

The newspaper *Tertulia Patriótica de la Isla de León* includes very interesting news about the fate of don Juan Tupac-Amaro, a descendent of the ancient Incas of Peru, who after thirty-seven years of imprisonment in the Ceuta presidio was just freed by the citizens of good principles there. The facts are the following.

D. José Gabriel Tupac-Amaro, don Juan's older brother, rose the banner of insurrection in Peru in 1781, for well-known and just causes. "Long Live the King and Death to Bad Government" was the warning signal then used by malcontents in Spain and the Americas. Tupac Amaru followed this norm, seeking not independence and the freedom of his country but instead relief from the privations and burdens that they suffered. For this, they took up arms.

Backed by a numerous contingent, Tupac Amaru made rapid progress. . . .

Juan Tupac-Amaro was not made for war nor for revolutions. While his comrades grappled in the insurrection, he remained calmly at home, taking care of his family and not taking part in the insurrection. Thugs, however, arrested him without any grounds other than the two brothers' fraternity and the assumption that Juan Bautista at least knew about the project and was thus guilty of not having informed on him. After seven months of imprisonment and an investigation, no proof was uncovered and he was freed.

Juan was enjoying his freedom surrounded by his family when the Viceroy received a Royal Order to detain and send all the Tupac-Amaros, their women and children, and anyone believed to be descended from the Incas of Peru to Spain, under the supervision of His Majesty. Juan was the first victim of this harsh expatriation: arrested and taken to Callao with his family and many relatives, they arrived exhausted after this long and painful march, in which his 125-year-old uncle Don N. died; they were placed on different ships and for reasons I don't know don Juan was separated from his wife and children. He reached Cádiz in 1785 and only then learned that his family had died in the journey.[1]

To console him for such a great loss they stuck him in the San Sebastián Castle, shackled. For three years he suffered in this prison, never having been tried or sentenced or even interrogated by the court. At this point he was confined to Ceuta with an order that in substance is as follows: "Juan Tupac Amaru is one of those who came from Peru, according to the list sent to the Ministry of the Indies; and His Majesty desires that this individual reside and stay in this plaza [Ceuta] for as long as royal will deems, providing him 6 reales daily for food." The date was 1788, Ministry of War. Subsequently, another order was dispatched, increasing his pension to 8 reales, as this was the sum offered to Tupac Amaru's comrades.

He was in jail from 1783 until March 1820, thirty-seven years of imprisonment. The will of King Charles III was the law that imposed this sentence on an innocent American. The Cádiz Courts abolished this abuse, converting the Absolute Monarchy into a Moderate Monarchy. Nonetheless, he still faced

---

[1]   This is incorrect. Juan Bautista and his wife Susan Aguirre traveled on the same boat, where she died. They did not have children.

obstacles, although the sovereign division of powers provided citizens the best safeguard against judiciary despotism by the Crown. Nonetheless, Tupac Amaru was excluded [from the amnesty], despite imploring his case. His only hope was the philanthropy of Ceuta's Liberals, that they would recognize the injuries and injustice of thirty-seven years of imprisonment for one person. The acclaim for their action in freeing him will extend to the most remote climes; the blessings for his liberators will not be temporary, but will echo forever in the land where this venerable old man was born: and all sensitive hearts will hope that these sentiments and virtues developed in that corner of the Kingdom of Fez [Morocco] will spread through all of Africa, desolated more by debilitating vices than by the wild animals and plagues that they contain.

Diario Constitucional Político y Mercantil de Barcelona
February 6, 1821, #37

8. ALGECIRAS

AMNESTY REJECTED, 1822

This brief document from 1822 no doubt crushed Juan Bautista's hopes. It listed Durán Martel and him as recipients of the amnesty but then noted at the bottom that Juan Bautista was exempt from this benefit. He learned elsewhere that it was because he had been sentenced by King Charles III so many decades previously. In other words, he had been imprisoned too long to receive this specific pardon.

List of the American individuals eligible for the amnesty law, who from the port of Gibraltar should return to their family home.

1. Father Don Antonio Herrera
2. Father Don José Ximénez
3. Father Fr. Marcos Durán Martel
4. Officer Don Mariano Zubieta
5. *Paisano* [Civilian] Don Juan Tupac-amaro
6. D. Don Manuel Sauri
7. Note. From outside sources we know that don Mariano Sánchez, also eligible for the amnesty, is a prisoner and will not be aided . . . Cádiz May 4, 1822, Barreda

Note. Tupac Amaru is not included in the assignation of amnesty.

Archivo General de Indias, Ultramar, Legajo 847, No. 39/25

9. TUPAC AMARU TO BERNARDINO RIVADAVIA AND HIS RESPONSE, 1822

Tupac Amaru and Durán Martel arrived in Buenos Aires on October 15, 1822. A week later, Juan Bautista presented this petition to Bernardino Rivadavia, the Minister of Government of Buenos Aires (Argentina did not unify until 1826), requesting accommodations and a pension. Rivadavia granted them to him two days later, leading some to assume that they had already discussed the arrangement.[1]

Tupac Amaru to Bernardino Rivadavia
October 22, 1822

Your Excellency:

Don Juan Tupamaro, from Canasicanchi, Cuzco Province, declares to your excellency with due respect, the following: That on October 15 of this year he arrived in the capital [Buenos Aires] from Gibraltar, after coming over from Ceuta, where the despotic and tyrannical Spanish government had sentenced him to civil death as a result of the so-called raucous rebellion of Peru overseen by his brother D. José Gabriel in 1781. He has suffered all types of mistreatment and privations ever since. It is not his intention, your excellency, to provide an account of the painful imprisonments that he has suffered in the dilated time of forty years, but it is crucial that he tell about the loss of his dear brother, destroyed by four horses; the death of our cousin, quartered, his limbs displayed in different points; the assassination of his sister-in-law, Tupac Amaru's wife; the death of our sixteen-year-old cousin on a scaffold; the death of our two nephews, both minors, sent to Europe, one of them dying during the navigation and the other in Madrid; the death during the trip to Spain of so many innocent people whose only crime was being members and dependents of the Tupac Amaru family, persecuted and annihilated for this. This array of evils afflicted his anguished heart, surrounded by his adversaries, but it was even more painful when he contemplated that his brother and family's sacrifice had been in vain, and that Despotism had rebuilt its throne with even more rigor on top of his relatives' cadavers, under the barbarous and inhumane whims of Charles III and his descendants, and that the weight of the chains had only become heavier for the indigenous people of this vast and fertile land, in proportion to the greed of the barbaric representatives of Despotism.

---

[1]   On October 28, the Buenos Aires newspaper *Argos* reported that "the government has granted Tupa-Camaro a 30-pesos pension and housing, on the condition that he write in his own handwriting the text that he presented to the government relating his sufferings. This along with the decree should be archived in the biography section." *Argos*, #81, October 26, 1822.

But, oh Lord!, how delighted he was when he first heard the echoes of the proclamation of freedom across the American continent; that was when he returned to life, despite the many years and the work that had exhausted him: a new hope was reborn in his heart, seeing that the peaceful children of the Sun [the Incas] became acquainted with their rights and duties, shielded by the high dignity of free men granted by God and Nature, and that the chains had been broken forever. Animated by this cheerful idea, his overwhelmed soul harkened back centuries, and he resolved to return to his beloved fatherland, as soon as the well-known circumstances allowed, overlooking the discomfort and risks in a long ocean voyage, for which he counted on minimal comfort. He ultimately overcame these obstacles and managed to set foot on the land where he had the good fortune to be born and thus he is here, delighted to live with his compatriots, under the protection of a free and benevolent government that knows how to balance justice and equity.

Therefore, To Your Excellency, he pleads that, in light of his long suffering, 85 years of age, and his penurious situation, that you grant him accommodations and some help for his maintenance and propriety, while providence allows him to return to his country of birth.

This is the grace that he hopes to receive from the benevolent heart of Your Excellency, which is so characteristic.

Buenos Ayres, October 22, 1822

Juan Tupa Maro

Boleslao Lewin, *La rebelión de Túpac Amaru*. Buenos Aires: Hachette, 1957, 901–902.

In response to a petition presented by Don Juan Tupa Amaru in which, describing his long suffering, he requests the Government's protection, it has today decreed the following:

The Hospital Administrator, following the verbal instructions given yesterday, will provide complete room and board to Don Juan Tupa Amaro, who will also receive 30 pesos monthly for his personal expenses, provided from this point forward by the government's reserve funds. Both the housing and the pension will be provided as long as he resides in this capital. Communicate this resolution to the Ministry of Finance and the Hospital administrator. The Secretary of Government Minister has the honor of communicating this to the Ministry of Finance.

Bernardino Rivadavia

Buenos Aires

October 24, 1822

Francisco Loayza, ed. *Cuarenta años de cautiverio (Memorias del Inka Juan Bautista Túpac Amaru)*. Lima: Editorial Domingo Miranda, 1941, 71–72.

10. LETTER TO SIMÓN BOLÍVAR, 1825

In this poignant letter to the South American Liberator, Simón Bolívar, Juan Bautista asks for his support to return to Peru, his homeland and the land of the Incas. Peru's independence fighters had defeated the Spanish in the Battle of Ayacucho on December 9, 1824 and in 1825 Bolívar took a victory tour of southern Peru, including Cuzco (June 25–July 26). It is unclear if the letter ever reached Bolívar. Juan Bautista never received a response.

Buenos Aires
May 15, 1825

To the Honorable Sir Don Simón Bolívar, Liberator of Peru

If it has been a duty of friends of the Inca Homeland [Cuzco], the memories of which are among my warmest and respectful, to congratulate the Hero of Colombia and the Liberator of the vast countries of South America, I myself have a double motivation to express that my heart is filled with the highest jubilation. I have made it to the age of eighty-six, despite great hardships and threats to my life, to see consummated the great and always just struggle that will grant us the full enjoyment of our rights and liberty. This was the aim of Don José Gabriel Tupac Amaru, my venerated and affectionate brother and martyr of the Peruvian Empire, whose blood irrigated the soil to make the land fertile, so that the Great Bolívar could pick with his valiant and very generous hands the best fruit. I also aimed to free our people and although I did not have the glory of spilling the blood of my Inca forefathers which runs through my veins, I spent forty years in exile and in prison. This was the fruit of my just desire and my efforts to take back the freedom and rights that those tyrannical usurpers took with such cruelty. I, in the name of the spirits of my sacred ancestors, congratulate the American Spirit of the Century . . .

God is very just. May God favor all the undertakings of the immortal Don Simón Bolívar and crown his efforts with laurels of immortal glory, keeping him safe for the consolation of the numerous family that still laments the unjust death of their parents. If it were possible, may God also reunite the only traces that Providence has kept of the Incas of Peru, with the cold ashes of their venerated ancestors.

I, sir, considering the series of hardships that to this day I remember, harbor in my heart the sweet prospect of breathing the air of my homeland and I am confident that the great Bolívar will fulfill this dream, as a man of a grand and generous soul. He only needs to facilitate my journey through Upper Peru, for which nature is calling me, despite having been so fortunate since arriving on the shores of Buenos Aires. The incalculable grief and hardships I have suffered would seem as nothing if, before my eyes close, I might see my Liberator, and with this comfort I could go to my grave.

Juan Bautista Tupamaro

CDIP, *La rebelión de Túpac Amaru*, II, 3, doc. 327, 908–909. Lima, 1972

11. ANGELIS, "PRELIMINARY DISCOURSE TO THE TUPAC AMARU REBELLION," 1836

Italian intellectual Pedro de Angelis arrived in Argentina in 1827 and became an important ideologue of the caudillo Juan Manuel Rosas. He published widely, including the first set of documents about the Tupac Amaru Rebellion. His assessment of Juan Bautista as an impostor influenced historians and writers for decades, if not centuries.

In this text, Angelis stresses the cruelty of Spanish repression against the Tupac Amaru Rebellion and incorrectly claims that only one Tupac Amaru family member survived, Fernando, the youngest son of Tupac Amaru and Micaela Bastidas. After witnessing the brutal executions of his parents, Fernando was sent to Spain on the *Alcántara*, nearly drowned in a shipwreck, and died in Madrid in 1798. Both footnotes are from Angelis.

Areche, Medina, and Mata Linares, perpetrators of so many atrocities, have received honors and applause; but the state of their victims, their last cries, their throbbing limbs, their bodies destroyed by torture, are memories that are not easily forgotten and should be perpetuated in history, their names added to the historical registrar of abhorrence.[1] The annals of history offer few examples of such horrifying butchery. Not only were Tupac Amaru, his wife, son, brothers, uncles, in-laws, and confidantes tortured and executed, but all of their relatives, no matter how distant the relation, were proscribed. Only one eleven-year-old child was saved, Tupac Amaru's son, who had to witness the torture of his parents and relatives. He was sent to Spain where he died shortly afterwards. Therefore, we must consider apocryphal the title of "fifth grandson of the Last Emperor of Peru" that Juan Bautista Tupamaru assumed in order to get a lifelong pension from the Government of Buenos Aires.[2]

Pedro de Angelis, "Discurso preliminar a la revolución de Tupac-Amaru." In *Colección de obras y documentos relativos a la historia antigua y moderna de las provincias de Río de la Plata, ilustrados con notas y disertaciones por Pedro Angelis*, tomo V, pp. i-viii.

Buenos Aires: Imprenta del Estado, 1836.

---

[1] When Visitador Areche, watching Tupac Amaru's execution from the window of what had been the Jesuit College, saw that the four horses could not detach the poor soul's limbs, he ordered that he be beheaded. And they finished off Tupac Amaru's wife by "kicking her in the stomach." *Horresco referens!*

[2] The title of the pamphlet that this impostor published in Buenos Aires is: *El dilatado cautiverio bajo el gobierno español de Juan Bautista Tupamaru, quinto nieto del último Emperador del Perú.*

12. EXCERPTS FROM CLEMENTS MARKHAM, *TRAVELS IN PERU AND INDIA*, 1862

Clements Markham was an English geographer and explorer who wrote influential histories of Peru and accounts of his travels there. In this 1862 book, he reproduces Angelis's false claim that Juan Bautista was an impostor.

A person calling himself Juan Bautista Tupac Amaru, and professing to have been one of the sufferers, printed a pamphlet which was deposited in the archives of Buenos Ayres. In it he relates the tale of his miseries in uncouth Spanish. He says that he beheld his fettered mother perish of thirst on the road to Lima, in presence of guards who turned a deaf ear to her cries for water. He saw his faithful wife die on board the ship, without being allowed length of chain enough to approach her. During an imprisonment of forty years at Ceuta, the sentries never relaxed their cruelties until the ministry which came into power in Spain, after the military movement of 1820, set the few survivors at liberty.

It is now confidently asserted that the author of this pamphlet was an impostor. He came to Buenos Ayres in 1822, and the republican government granted him a house, and a pension for life of 30 dollars a month.

Clements R. Markham, *Travels in Peru and India*. London: John Murray, Albemarle Street, 1862, p. 168.

FURTHER READING AND SOURCES

I include in this essay sources that I used for preparing this book and those that might be of interest for additional reading. My research for this project ranged from the very specific (what color uniforms did soldiers in Ceuta wear?) to the broad (the Mediterranean in the Napoleonic Wars). For this guide, I have favored English over Spanish sources.

JUAN BAUTISTA TUPAC AMARU

Juan Bautista Tupac Amaru's memoirs are the key to this project and to understanding him and his era. I leaned heavily on Francisco Loayza's 1941 edition, loaded with primary documents and insights (Francisco Loayza, ed. *Cuarenta años de cautiverio [Memorias del Inka Juan Bautista Túpac Amaru]*. Lima: Editorial Domingo Miranda, 1941). As we point out in the comic, Loayza and his daughter María Emilia conducted research for several years in the Archivo General de Indias in the 1930s, when he was the Peruvian consul in Seville. Numerous editions have appeared since then, each providing additional information. Eduardo Astesano's is excellent, particularly on Juan Bautista's curious reception in Buenos Aires (*Juan Bautista de America: El Rey Inca de Manuel Belgrano*. Buenos Aires: Ediciones Castañeda, 1979).

Multi-volume document collections on the Tupac Amaru Rebellion and the 150th anniversary of Peruvian independence contain important papers on Juan Bautista (*Colección Documental de la Independencia del Perú*, vol. 2, *La rebelión de Túpac Amaru*. 4 vols. Lima: Comisión Nacional del Sesquicentenario de la Independencia del Perú, 1971; *Colección documental del bicentenario de la revolución emancipadora de Túpac Amaru*. Lima, Peru: Comisión Nacional del Bicentenario de la Rebelión Emancipadora de Túpac Amaru, 1980–1982).

TUPAC AMARU AND CUZCO

Much has been written about the Tupac Amaru Rebellion. For two recent overviews, see Sergio Serulnikov, *Revolution in the Andes: The Age of Túpac Amaru* (Durham, NC: Duke University Press, 2013) and Charles F. Walker, *The Tupac Amaru Rebellion* (Cambridge, MA: The Belknap Press of Harvard University Press, 2014). Scarlett O'Phelan Godoy is outstanding for the long history of rebellions in the Andes (*Rebellions and Revolts in Eighteenth-Century Peru and Upper Peru*. Cologne: Bohlau, 1985). Ward Stavig sheds light on Cuzco (*The World of Túpac Amaru: Conflict, Community, and Identity in Colonial Peru*. Lincoln: University of Nebraska Press, 1999), and David Garrett on the indigenous elite (*Shadows of Empire: The Indian Nobility of Cusco, 1750–1825*. Cambridge, UK: Cambridge University Press, 2005).

Ward Stavig and Ella Schmidt compiled a valuable document collection in English (*The Tupac Amaru and Catarista Rebellions. An Anthology of Sources*. Introduction by Charles F. Walker. Indianapolis, IN: Hackett, 2008). I published a bibliographic essay available online which I update every few years: Charles Walker, "The

Tupac Amaru Rebellion" (*Oxford Bibliographies in Latin American Studies*, edited by Ben Vinson III. New York: Oxford University Press, 2016). On travel in the eighteenth-century Andes, "Concolorcorvo" is a rich contemporary fictional account by Alonso Carrió de la Vandera (Concolorcorvo, *El Lazarillo: A Guide for Inexperienced Travelers Between Buenos Aires and Lima*, 1773. Translated by Walter D. Kline. Bloomington: Indiana University Press, 1965).

LIMA TO CÁDIZ

I have written about eighteenth-century Lima and Callao (*Shaky Colonialism: The 1746 Earthquake-Tsunami in Lima, Peru and Its Long Aftermath*. Durham, NC: Duke University Press, 2008), and I also benefitted from Tamara Walker's *Exquisite Slaves: Race, Status, and Clothing in Colonial Lima* (Cambridge, UK: Cambridge University Press, 2017). For a variety of documents and perspectives on Lima, see Carlos Aguirre and Charles Walker, *The Lima Reader* (Durham, NC: Duke University Press, 2017). I learned a great deal about scientific expeditions and Joseph Dombey, who was on board the *El Peruano* with Juan Bautista, in Arthur Robert Steele, *Flowers for the King: The Expedition of Ruiz and Pavon and the Flora of Peru* (Durham, NC: Duke University Press, 1964), which led me to Dombey's self-aggrandizing account. Dombey never mentions the shackled prisoners but claims that he helped defeat the Tupac Amaru Rebellion ("Historical Account of Jos. Dombey, Translated from the French of M. Deleuze (Concluded)," *The Belfast Monthly Magazine* 2, no. 7, February 28, 1809).

On Rio de Janeiro, I found valuable Mariz de Carvalho Soares, *People of Faith: Slavery and African Catholics in Eighteenth-Century Rio de Janeiro* (Durham, NC: Duke University Press, 2011). From Rio, the next stop for Juan Bautista was Cádiz. The internet is a great source for historical images and maps of both of these beautiful port cities. One topic I knew little about was the boats used to cross the Atlantic. The essays in Enrique Manera Regueyra's *El buque en la armada española* provide a wealth of information and images on Spanish vessels (Madrid: Sílex, 1999). Although focused on an earlier period, Pablo E. Pérez-Mallaína, *Men of the Sea: Daily Life on the Indies Fleets in the Sixteenth Century* (Baltimore: Johns Hopkins University Press, 2005), is a fantastic introduction to the Atlantic crossings.

CEUTA

I knew nothing about Ceuta and relied heavily on the guidance of colleagues, who (easily) convinced me that I needed to visit. In his novel, *La Ciudad Reversible*, Antonio Carmona Portillo vividly portrays the 1790–91 Moroccan siege of Ceuta, which Juan Bautista experienced (Málaga: Editorial Sarriá, 2008). Antonio Garrido Aranda's article, "Hacer morir en Ceuta: Los ajusticiados en los siglos XVIII y XIX," provides a grim portrait of prisoners' lives in Ceuta (Luis Palacio Bañuelos, ed., *De puntillas por la historia*. Córdoba: Universidad de Córdoba, 1997, 106–120). Other key secondary works included Antonio Carmona Portillo, *Historia de Una Ciudad Fronteriza: Ceuta en la Edad Moderna* (Málaga: Editorial Sarriá, 1997), as well as his *La vida cotidiana en Ceuta a través de los tiempos* (Ceuta: Instituto de Estudios Ceutíes, 2007); Manuel Gordillo Osuna, *Geografía Urbana de Ceuta* (Madrid: Instituto de Estudios Africanos, 1972); and, for a rich collection of maps and images, Juan B. Vilar and María José Vilar, *Límites, Fortificaciones y Evolución Urbana de Ceuta (Siglos XV–XX)* (Ciudad Autónoma de Ceuta: Consejería de Educación y Cultura, 2002). On sailors and the transmission of news, gossip, and rumors, see Julius S. Scott, *The Common Wind: Afro-American Currents in the Age of the Haitian Revolution* (London: Verso, 2018) and Nathan

Perl-Rosenthal, *Citizen Sailors: Becoming American in the Age of Revolution* (Cambridge, MA: The Belknap Press of Harvard University Press, 2015).

BUENOS AIRES AND ARGENTINA

Argentina has enjoyed a renaissance of fantastic social history on the independence era. I relied on Gabriel Di Meglio's *1816: La verdadera trama de la independencia* (Buenos Aires: Planeta, 2016). See also Raúl Fradkin, ed., *¿Y el pueblo dónde está?: Contribuciones para una historia popular de la revolución de independencia en el Río de la Plata* (Buenos Aires: Prometeo Libros, 2015), and Klaus Gallo, *The Struggle for an Enlightened Republic: Buenos Aires and Rivadavia* (London: Institute for the Study of the Americas, 2006). Bartolomé Mitre's classic work is still fundamental (*Historia de Belgrano y de la independencia argentina.* Buenos Aires: El Ateneo, 2014 [1858–59]), while Tulio Halperín Donghi's *Politics, Economics and Society in Argentina in the Revolutionary Era* (Cambridge, UK: Cambridge University Press, 1975) continues to be an excellent source.

On the Incas and Argentine nationalist history, see Jesús Díaz Caballero, "Incaísmo as the First Guiding Fiction in the Emergence of the Creole Nation in the Provinces of Río de la Plata," *Journal of Latin American Cultural Studies* 17, no. 1 (2008): 1–22; and, more generally for Inca utopianism, Alberto Flores Galindo, *In Search of an Inca: Identity and Utopia in the Andes* (edited and translated by Carlos Aguirre, Willie Hiatt, and Charles Walker. Cambridge, UK: Cambridge University Press, 2010).

SPAIN, SPANISH AMERICA, AND THE AGE OF REVOLUTION

For periodization and the warfare of the era, I consulted Mike Rapport, *The Napoleonic Wars: A Very Short Introduction* (Oxford: Oxford University Press, 2013). On the Cádiz Courts, Scott Eastman and Natalia Sobrevilla Perea provide important essays (*The Rise of Constitutional Government in the Iberian Atlantic World. The Impact of the Cádiz Constitution of 1812.* Tuscaloosa: University of Alabama Press, 2015). For Spain in this period I relied on Josep Fontana, *Historia de España: La época del Liberalismo,* vol. 6 (Barcelona: Editorial Planeta, 2018), and, for a comparative perspective, Josep Fradera, *The Imperial Nation: Citizens and Subjects in the British, French, Spanish, and American Empires* (Princeton, NJ: Princeton University Press, 2018). See also Jesús Astigarraga, ed., *The Spanish Enlightenment Revisited* (Oxford: Oxford Studies in the Enlightenment, 2015).

Two recent books on the Wars of Independence served me well: Anthony McFarlane, *War and Independence in Spanish America* (New York: Routledge, 2013), and Brian R. Hamnett, *The End of Iberian Rule on the American Continent, 1770–1830* (Cambridge, UK: Cambridge University Press, 2017).

DURÁN MARTEL AND THE HUÁNUCO REBELLION OF 1812

Durán Martel deserves a full biography and the Huánuco uprising more attention. The key starting place is the *Colección Documental de la Independencia del Perú* document collection. Ella Dunbar Temple provides a great introduction ("Prólogo," *Conspiraciones y rebeliones en el siglo XIX. La Revolución de Huánuco, Panataguas y Huamalíes. Colección Documental de la Independencia del Perú* 1, III. Lima: Comisión Nacional del Sesquicentenario de la Independencia del Perú, 1971, I–XCVII). Javier Campos y Fernández de Sevilla has published several informative articles, among them "Presencia de los agustinos en la revolución peruana de Huánuco," *Anuario Jurídico y Económico Escurialense* XLV (2012): 637–686.

SOURCES

Most of the information used for the graphic history came from Juan Bautista's memoirs. What follows are specific references used on individual pages of the comic, numbered by **page**. I have left out constitutions and treaties that are readily available online.

9, family tree: Adapted from Eulogio Zudaire, *Agustín de Jáuregui, virrey del Perú*. Pamplona, Spain: Diputación Foral de Navarra, Dirección de Turismo, Bibliotecas y Cultura Popular, 1971.

28, Dombey anecdote: "Historical Account of Jos. Dombey, Translated from the French of M. Deleuze (Concluded)," *The Belfast Monthly Magazine* 2, no. 7 (Feb. 28, 1809), 121.

36, shipwreck: Jorge Russo, "O San Pedro de Alcantara, 1786," Texas A&M Nautical Archaeology Program, accessed December 10, 2019, http://nautarch.tamu.edu/shiplab/baleal-ship-sanpedro.htm.

37, report from commander José de Córdoba, August 10, 1784: *Colección Documental de la Independencia del Perú*, Vol. 2, *La rebelión de Túpac Amaru*, 4 vols. (Lima: Comisión Nacional del Sesquicentenario de la Independencia del Perú, 1971, 2, 3), 427–428. (Reproduced in Primary Sources section).

37, dead: Francisco Loayza, ed., *Cuarenta años de cautiverio*. Lima: Editorial Domingo Miranda, 1941, pp. 148–149.

45, "Estado General de la Población de la Plaza de Ceuta en el año de 1787," Biblioteca Nacional de España.

48, Archivo Parroquial de Nuestra Señora de los Remedios, Padrones Parroquiales, Año 1812, Ceuta.

49, Archivo General de Ceuta, Fondo Carlos Posac Mon, Legajo 30, fotocopia de documento manuscrito de procedencia desconocida.

64, Durán Martel document: Ella Dunbar Temple, ed., *Conspiraciones y rebeliones en el siglo XIX. La Revolución de Huánuco, Panataguas y Huamalíes. Colección Documental de la Independencia del Perú 1* (III) (Lima: Comisión Nacional del Sesquicentenario de la Independencia del Perú, 1971, February 18, 1812), tomo 2, 65.

69, Archivo Parroquial de Nuestra Señora de los Remedios, Padrones Parroquiales, Año 1819, Ceuta.

71, Archivo General de Indias, Indiferente, Legajo 1351.

73, Lilly Library, Indiana University. Latin American Mss. Venezuela, Letter from Juan Germán Roscio, August 24, 1819.

75, *El Cetro Constitucional* (Madrid) #1, December 1820; *Miscelánea de Comercio, Política y Literatura* (Madrid) #333–334, January 26–27, 1821 (National Library of Spain).

76, exclusion from amnesty: Archivo General de Indias, Ultramar, Legajo 847, No. 39/25. (Reproduced in Primary Sources section).

77, *Retrieve, Lloyd's Register of British and Foreign Shipping* (London: W. Marchant, 1821), 8.

84, Arrival in Montevideo and Buenos Aires: *Archivo General de la Nación, Buenos Aires (AGN)*, Argentina, Sala X, 35-5-10, 1818–1822, Marina, Entradas de buques a ultramar, January 4, 1818 to December 29, 1822, #288 (October 28, 1822). Arrival of *Retrieve; AGN*, Sala III, Capitanía del puerto, caja 13, 1822 (carga).

88, Belgrano speech excerpted in *El Censor* (Buenos Aires) 55 (September 12, 1816), 5–6.

89, Criticism: Bartolomé Mitre, *Historia de Belgrano y de la independencia argentina*, vol. 2 (Buenos Aires: F. Lajouane, 1887), 435.

90, *Tupac-Amarú* [sic] *Drama en cinco actas. Año de 1821* (Buenos Aires: Facultad de Filosofía y Letras, Universidad de Buenos Aires, Instituto de Literatura

Argentina, Buenos Aires: Imprenta y Casa Editora "Coni," 1924); *Oración fúnebre de Tupac-Amaru; Publicada por Melchor Equazini* (Buenos Aires: Imprenta del Sol, 1816, and Lima: INC/Biblioteca Nacional, 1981, preliminary study by José Tamayo Herrera); *La Prensa Argentina. Seminario político y económico* (Buenos Aires), September 24, 1816 (Biblioteca de Mayo, tomo VII).

91, Petition to Rivadavia, Boleslao Lewin, *La rebelión de Túpac Amaru* (Buenos Aires: Hachette, 1957), 901–902; Rivadavia's decree, Francisco Loayza, ed., *Cuarenta años de cautiverio (Memorias del Inka Juan Bautista Túpac Amaru)* (Lima: Editorial Domingo Miranda, 1941), 71–72 (reproduced in Primary Sources section).

92, *Argos*, Buenos Aires, #81, October 26, 1822, p. 4; *Conduct of the British Consul-General Mr. Parish to Mr. Oughgan, Surgeon, a British Subject in Buenos Ayres* (London: J. Innes Printer, 1824).

93, *El Dilatado Cautiverio bajo del Gobierno Español de Juan Bautista Tupamaru, 5 nieto del Último Emperador del Perú* (Buenos Aires: Imprenta de los Niños Expósitos, 1825?).

94, Bolívar letter: *Colección Documental de la Independencia del Perú*, Vol. 2, *La rebelión de Túpac Amaru*, 4 vols. (Lima: Comisión Nacional del Sesquicentenario de la Independencia del Perú, 1971, 2, 3, doc. 327), 908–909.

100 & 101, Pedro de Angelis, "Discurso preliminar a la revolución de Tupac Amaru," in his *Colección de obras y documentos relativos a la historia antigua y moderna de las provincias de Río de la Plata* (Buenos Aires, Imprenta del Estado, 1836, tomo V).

102, Clements R. Markham, *Travels in Peru and India While Superintending the Collection of Chinchona Plants and Seeds in South America, and Their Introduction into India* (London: John Murray, Albedmarle Street, 1862), 168.

103, *La Estrella de Panamá*, November 25, 1880; *The Daily Star and Herald*, November 19, 1880.

104, Francisco Loayza, ed., *Cuarenta años de cautiverio (Memorias del Inka Juan Bautista Túpac Amaru)* (Lima: Editorial Domingo Miranda, 1941), 13–14.

105, Review by Calvert J. Winter, *Books Abroad* 18, no. 4 (Autumn, 1944): 375.

ACKNOWLEDGMENTS

Many people helped me on this project, aid that ranged from assisting me on research trips to answering random questions such as how high socks went on eighteenth-century prisoners (not very). Their generosity inspired me and made this book possible. Ari Kelman encouraged me from the start and offered consistently good advice. My concern when beginning the project was that I knew nothing about Ceuta, where Juan Bautista spent more than half of his long life. Antonio Garrido Aranda replied to my initial query enthusiastically, insisting that I visit Ceuta and putting me in touch with Antonio Carmona Portillo and José Luis Gómez Barceló. They proved crucial, answering dozens and dozens of emails. José Luis was a great host in my trip to Ceuta, showing me the archive, various historical sites, and the culinary scene. Antonio Carmona Portillo generously shared his vast knowledge of Ceuta's history, correcting my misunderstandings and, like José Luis, recommending articles and lending documents. I could not have done this without them. Father Javier Campos y Fernández de Sevilla enlightened me about the life and education of his fellow Augustinian, Friar Marcos Durán Martel. Luis Miguel Glave encouraged me throughout the project and provided me with key sources from the Archivo de Indias. Antonio Acosta also aided me in Sevilla.

One of the personal benefits of writing this book was returning to Tucumán and Buenos Aires and immersing myself in the great rethinking of nineteenth-century Argentina that has taken place in the last decade or so. I owe a great deal to Gabriel Di Meglio, who led me to period sources on Buenos Aires and guided me on the historiography, old and new. He received at least a dozen emails from me that promised to be my final request for assistance. Martín Bergel, Santiago Conti, Raúl Fradkin, Noemí Goldman, Mariana Katz, Pablo Ortemberg, and Fabio Wasserman also helped me on my quest for information about Juan Bautista Tupac Amaru and Argentina. Thanks to my brothers Raúl and Daniel Moeremans as well. Alex Borucki and Fabricio Prado tracked down shipping records so that I could be more precise about Juan Bautista and Durán Martel's journey from Algeciras to Buenos Aires, via Montevideo. Maritime history was a mystery to me, and I thank Bruce Castleman for his aid with additional shipping records and boat descriptions. Christian Rodríguez Aldana, Rosario Medina Montoya, and Ruth Borja Santa Cruz guided me on a fantastic tour of San Felipe Fortress in Callao.

Gabriel Paquette, Víctor Peralta, and Natalia Sobrevilla answered numerous inquiries about Spain in the period, while Ascensión Martínez Riaza shared documents about Francisco Loayza's 1930s research on Tupac Amaru in Seville. Marissa Bazán enlightened me about Huánuco 1812 and the role of Durán Martel. Stella Nair, Verónica Muñoz Nájar, and Tom Cummins answered questions about eighteenth-century Andean decor and drinking vessels, while Karina Fernández Gonzales tracked down documents in Lima. I also want to acknowledge Julio Aguilar, Priscilla Cisternas, Marcos Cueto, Greg Downs, Alejandro Gómez, Susan Miller, Margareth Najarro, Jorge Ortiz-Sotelo, Patricia Palma, Mike Saler, Marcel Velásquez Castro, and Adam Warren for their help.

María Teresa López Arandia of the Archivo de Indias expeditiously answered my query about Loayza's research, and the Lilly Library came to my aid rapidly with documents on Venezuela. The Biblioteca Nacional del Perú once again proved important and I want to thank Laura Martínez Silva for her guidance. I also used the fine collection at the Biblioteca Nacional of Argentina. I counted on two fabulous research assistants in Davis, Jacob Glazer and Mercedez Perucho. Karina Pacheco listened to my long stories about Juan Bautista and provided pictures of Cuzco monuments. Victoria Langland, Bruce Mannheim, and Ken Mills hosted my first talk about Juan Bautista, at the University of Michigan, and gave me wonderful advice and encouragement. Andrés Reséndez read the texts thoughtfully and shared his own considerable knowledge of transoceanic history and good writing. Carlos Aguirre and José Ragas listened, read, and guided me throughout the project, as did Zoila Mendoza. My children María and Samuel motivated me, even listening to a few of my stories.

Oxford University Press does not skimp on reviewers and I would like to acknowledge the insights and advice of the dozen colleagues or so who provided important feedback. Charles Cavaliere launched the project with a steady hand and strong sense of humor, and Susan Ferber saw it to the finish line with her incomparable editorial eye. I would also like to thank Melissa Yanuzzi of OUP and James Fraleigh for their help in the editing process. Liz Clarke is not only a superb artist but also a dream collaborator. Thanks, Liz, for your patience and creativity.

This book would not have been possible without the work of Francisco Loayza (1872–1963), who published Juan Bautista's memoirs in 1941. He was an indefatigable researcher and astute editor who deserves his own biography. Historians are not supposed to become enamored of their subjects, but I dedicate this book to Juan Bautista and Friar Marcos Durán Martel. Their endurance, loyalty to each other, and persistence in writing and publishing the memoirs inspired me for this book and beyond.